Bread Baking
for Beginners

The Essential Guide to Baking Kneaded Breads,
No-Knead Breads, and Enriched Breads

Bread
Baking

for

Beginners

⟫ BONNIE OHARA ⟪

Owner-Baker of Alchemy Bread Co.

callisto
publishing
an imprint of Sourcebooks

Copyright © 2018 by Callisto Publishing LLC
Cover and internal design © 2018 by Callisto Publishing LLC
Designer: Christopher T. Fong
Editor: Pippa White
Production Editor: Erum Khan
Photography © Paige Green, 2018
Food Stylist: Alysia Andriola

Callisto and the colophon are registered trademarks of Callisto Publishing LLC.

Published by Callisto Publishing LLC C/O Sourcebooks LLC
P.O. Box 4410, Naperville, Illinois 60567-4410
(630) 961-3900
callistopublishing.com

Printed and Bound In China
OGP 17

This book is dedicated to
my dear friend Jennifer Kara.

She was the first person who asked me to teach her about making bread, some five years ago. The sourdough starter I shared with her that day still lives in her kitchen, and she continues to bake for others and her family, a small ripple that made me feel that I could teach someone else what I have taught myself. She was my first regular subscriber, and she endlessly encouraged others to patronize my business, many of whom are now my friends. I will always be grateful for her encouragement and support.

Contents

PART TWO
RECIPES

Chapter Five: Enriched Breads: Brioche, Cinnamon Rolls, Babka, Challah, and Variations 81

Chapter Six: Breads with Pre-ferments and Sourdough Starter 111

Introduction

On most Saturdays at a quarter to noon, you will find me pulling out the last batch of baguettes from the hearth oven in the tiny kitchen of our little 1920s bungalow. A full day-and-night's labor comes to fruition; loaves in shades of sienna, mahogany, and deep gold glimmer in the sunlight. They are piled high on the kitchen table, on the built-in shelves, on the worktable, on the antique baker's table— every surface available. I pry open the old windows to let out the steam that has built up in the house, and as the scent of fresh baked bread wafts out the window, a line of customers begins to form at my front door, trailing out through the picket fence and down the street. While they wait, kids play cards, color with crayons, and look at picture books at the picnic tables. They play tag, running around in the wildflowers and clovers. Neighbors and friends swap stories as the line grows, and I wrap up baguettes and loaves, labeling each one carefully. Within an hour or two, all of the loaves have gone to new

homes in our community. It always gives me a special feeling when I finally rest after a long day, imagining all those loaves of bread ending up becoming part of a nice meal. I picture the baguettes on a cheese plate shared with friends, taken on picnics, going into lunchboxes, stuffed into backpacks on long hikes and adventures, nibbled on by babies' tiny teeth, or shared with extended family on holidays. It's still the same feeling I had the first time I shared a loaf I had made with my family or a friend.

Baking bread to share with others is the most elemental and nourishing connection we can create with those we love: our family, our children, and our neighborhood. As dreamy as that seems, my bread journey began for much more practical reasons—simply that we didn't have enough money for food, and I knew that the only way to stretch our budget would be if I started making more of our essentials from scratch. I borrowed some bread-baking books from the library, invested in a 25-pound bag of flour, and started trying to teach myself to bake for my family. Those first loaves were not beautiful, but the kids and I would sit on the floor next to the warmth of the oven and watch as the bread

baked. Then they would tear a loaf apart while it was still warm, the steam rising in front of their joyous faces. They didn't care that my loaves weren't perfect, only that we had something to share. Each loaf that I made was only marginally better than the previous one, but each small amount of improvement continued to feed my hopes that I could make a better loaf of bread—one I could be proud of. I continued biking to the library, kids in tow, to check out more and more baking books, and slowly, as I absorbed knowledge, practiced, and learned through trial and error, I became completely obsessed. My scrappy loaves began to shape up into something wonderful. I kept notebooks full of scribblings about the times, temperatures, weather, and anything else I could think of that might affect my process. Over time, I began to make bread that was reliably good, and I began to share it with people outside of my family. More and more friends began asking to be added to the "the bread list," a notebook where I would write down their names. My list started out with four names on it, but through word of mouth I quickly found myself with a list of 64 names. I began to realize it was time to turn what had been a simple attempt to feed my family into a tiny business. Some eight years after those very first loaves, I have a thriving, tiny cottage bakery with hundreds of regular customers and a wonderful community—and even enough money to go grocery shopping.

I loved learning how to bake bread using a book, but one of the things I discovered was that there was not just one book that would teach me—it took about 20 different books, with me getting different pieces of information from each, in order to learn everything I needed to know. Another thing I noticed whenever I cracked open a new bread book was that the introduction waxed long about the prestigious education the author had received at expensive cooking schools, and his trips around Europe to try all of the breads there, or her connections to famous chefs, as well as apprenticeships at famous bakeries. There I was with no means and no money, in a small town with no bread bakery, reading about those magical stories. I knew none of those routes would be an option for me. Another thing I found when reading different baking books was that the books aimed at beginners didn't take the reader seriously enough, and they didn't give me the information I needed to troubleshoot mistakes, make progress, and succeed. The books aimed at professionals, on the other hand, had tons of great information, but they were just too overwhelming for a beginner like me, who simply wanted to make my first few loaves of edible bread.

> Baking bread to share with others is the most elemental and nourishing connection we can create with those we love: our family, our children, and our neighborhood.

With all of that in mind, I present you with this book. While I can't regale you with tales of trips around the world, I hope I can inspire you to make something out of what you have, even if what you have is almost nothing. You can make a positive impact wherever you live, even if it isn't quite Paris or San Francisco. What I hope to do with this book is take you seriously from the start, give you the knowledge to succeed, and grow with you as you advance. We will fully cover all of the parts of the bread-baking process at the outset, so you know what you are getting into, and I will give you the simple tools that professionals use so you have good habits from the start. This book begins with a minimalist formula and advances as you practice, so you can build your confidence with each new skill. Each chapter of recipes will add new techniques to the ones you learned in the chapter before, empowering you gradually, instead of overwhelming you.

I truly believe that you can teach yourself to bake, just as I did, with this book as your guide. Let's begin!

—*Bonnie Ohara*

PART ONE

THE PROCESS OF BAKING BREAD

Chapter One

How Bread Is Formed

Baking bread is such an elemental process, I can't help but feel it is a deep, meditative connection to ages gone by. Combining wheat—the very essence of the earth—with water, salt from the sea, yeast from the air, and fire creates an alchemy that transforms the individual parts into much more than the whole. After baking so many loaves of bread, I now understand why all those scriptures, poems, stories, and fables make so much of bread and its importance to civilization and humanity. The truth of bread is that it requires a community and deep roots to exist. The farmer, the miller, the baker, and society itself, all working together toward a common goal. It is a beautiful ode to humankind and our ability to create magic with our own hands.

Even from a scientific perspective, the baking of bread is fascinating. Proteins in flour are hydrated by water; strengthened by salt; developed by mixing, kneading, or folding; fermented with yeast; and finally, baked into something completely delicious. What is most important to understand is that bread is a living thing, and working with a living thing (much like working with plants, children, or animals) requires developing your intuition through practice and, even more importantly, patience and adaptability.

Ingredients

Making a loaf of bread requires very few ingredients, so if you use the best quality you can find, you'll end up with better-tasting bread, but starting with what you have is all you truly need. Let's go over some specifics:

WATER: Hydration is critical for dough. If your tap water is acceptable to drink, it will be just fine for making bread. However, tap water high in chlorine can have a negative effect on a new sourdough starter. If you simply fill a pitcher from the tap and let it sit out overnight, the chlorine will evaporate. Temperature is another key factor in bread baking, so the temperature of your water is important (see Temperature Calculation on page 21).

SALT: In bread baking, salt performs the important function of adding strength to dough. It also slows or inhibits the fermentation process, which lets the dough develop structure and flavor over time. Any baker who forgets the salt will have the unpleasant experience of dealing with gooey, sticky dough and will end up with a poorly flavored loaf of bread. Use whatever salt you like or already have in your home. I like to use sea salt, personally, but I have made bread with all kinds of salt (even with saltwater collected directly from the sea) with successful results.

FLOUR: As the heart and soul of bread, the type of flour you use will make a difference in the bread you bake. Pay attention to the amount of protein in the flour. The higher the protein, the more gluten there is in the flour, which you need to develop the structure of the bread.

- Pastry or cake flour has very low protein.
- All-purpose flour has medium protein.
- Bread flour has high protein.

Every brand of flour will have varying qualities within these levels of protein and gluten. Note, though, that it's not necessary to buy the most expensive flour to make quality bread, and it's not absolutely necessary to use bread flour in these recipes. Even though bread flour is specifically made for bread, I call for all-purpose flour in most of the recipes in this book because it's easy to find and I've had a lot of success using it. I feel that one of the best brands to use is King Arthur unbleached all-purpose flour. Although it's all-purpose flour, it is higher in protein than other brands, is of good quality, and is easily accessible at most stores. Bob's Red Mill is a wonderful choice for whole-wheat flour and for a wide variety of other whole-grain flours. They can also be found in most large grocery stores.

YEAST: This is the magic ingredient that makes bread dough rise. Yeast occurs naturally in the air, and we'll use that natural yeast for breads made with a levain or sourdough starter. You can also buy commercially made yeast at the store. The two most commonly found types of yeast are active dry yeast and instant yeast. Instant yeast is what I always recommend, as it is a more stable product and can be used without being proofed to make sure it's alive. Instant yeast also delivers more consistent results and is used by most professionals. I like to buy yeast in a large, 2-pound bag because I make a lot of bread (you can find these at Costco, restaurant supply stores, and some larger groceries), but you can find it in 4-ounce and 8-ounce packages, too, which will work for anyone starting out. Once the package is open, I transfer my yeast to a zip-top bag and place it in the door of my refrigerator, which keeps it cool and easy to find. As you start making more bread, you will quickly find that you'll need more yeast than those individual packets provide.

Working with Whole-Grain Flour

Unlike all-purpose flour, whole-grain flour contains the germ and bran of the grain. These are full of fiber and nutritious, but they also increase the density and heaviness of bread. Working with whole-grain flours also requires more water to hydrate the absorbent bran, and extra consideration to the dough, as the bran can tear the gluten and make it difficult to develop the dough.

⊰⊱ Key Terminology ⊰⊱

Here is a list of terms I will use throughout the book. Feel free to refer back to this list at any point as a helpful refresher.

BENCH REST: Resting and relaxing the dough on the work surface before shaping.

BIGA: A stiff pre-ferment made of flour, water, and yeast.

BANNETON: Cane basket for proofing dough.

BATARD: An oval or football-shaped loaf.

BOULE: A round loaf.

COUCHE: A large piece of linen cloth that can be folded and creased around proofing loaves.

CRUMB: The interior structure of a loaf.

ENRICHED DOUGH: A dough that contains "rich" ingredients, like eggs, butter, oil, or sugar.

FERMENTATION: The process in which yeast converts sugars into carbon dioxide, creating air pockets in the dough.

GLUTEN: Protein in wheat that creates the elastic texture of dough.

GRIGNE: The "ear" or little lip of crust that rises away from the baked loaf along the score.

HYDRATION: The quantity of liquid in a dough relative to the amount of flour.

INSTANT YEAST: Instant yeast comes in granules, which don't need to be "proofed" before you use them. It has a high absorption rate, which makes it easier to use than active dry yeast.

KNEADING: Working a dough by hand to develop the strength in the dough.

LAME: A handy tool with a razor blade on one end for scoring bread.

OVEN SPRING: The final, dramatic rise of the loaf as it bakes in the oven.

POOLISH: A liquid pre-ferment that is usually equal parts water and flour with a small bit of yeast.

PROOF: The time when the final dough is rising in its final shape.

SCALING: Weighing out ingredients using a kitchen scale or weighing pieces of dough before shaping them.

An Overview of the Process

Basic bread baking follows a set of predictable steps. Here I'll briefly walk you through each step, and you'll learn why each one affects the final outcome of the loaf. You will learn more about how to perform each step within the recipes, but in order to set you up for success, I want you to have an overview of the bread-baking process and an understanding of the role each step plays within it.

Scaling → Mixing → Kneading and Folding →
Rising or Bulk Fermentation → Shaping → Proofing → Baking → Cooling

SCALING: This is the starting point. Weigh out each ingredient, make sure the water is the correct temperature, and set out all of your equipment. Being organized and prepared to bake makes the process go more smoothly. When baking, improper or inconsistent measurements and temperatures create inconsistent results, and it will be difficult to pinpoint what went wrong and learn from your mistakes. Consistency from the start is the ultimate ally of the bread baker.

MIXING: Combine all of the ingredients until the dough is hydrated and there are no dry spots. This begins the development of the gluten in the dough. An undermixed dough will have clumps of flour, unincorporated salt, and inconsistently mixed yeast, resulting in uneven fermentation and unappetizing clumps of ingredients in the final loaf. Proper mixing will create an even, homogenous dough that is soft and easy to work with. Mixing also creates friction, just like folding and kneading do, so a good thorough mix will kick-start the development process.

KNEADING AND FOLDING: Stretching or folding the dough creates strength and structure in the gluten network, and it's this strength that allows the bread to form properly. A loaf that hasn't had adequate gluten development will be difficult to shape, won't hold its shape in the oven, and will result in a flat loaf that won't rise. Dough with great gluten development will be strong, stretchy, and easy to shape. It will rise high in the oven and hold its shape.

RISING OR BULK FERMENTATION: The initial rise (called bulk fermentation by professionals) is when the yeast gets to work, eating the sugars and starches in the dough and turning them into gases, which fill the dough with air. These air pockets create flavor and lightness in the final loaf of bread. An insufficient rise will result in a loaf that is lacking in flavor, with a dense crumb. It will likely be heavy, like a brick. A well-fermented loaf, on the other hand, will have a great, full flavor and an airy crumb.

A piece of well
fermented dough
will have enough air
bubbles inside to
make it float; if it sinks
give it a bit more
time to rise

SHAPING: The act of giving form and structure to the dough is when the final shape of the loaf is determined. The tension built in the shaping process helps the loaf "spring" in the oven. (This is how professional bakers describe the additional rise of the bread while it bakes.) Shaping without enough tension results in a loaf that is flat, lacking in volume, and awkwardly formed. In this case, the overall rise suffers. A well-shaped loaf with adequate tension will rise tall and look beautiful. Dough can be formed into many shapes, and in this book we'll shape dough into boules, batards, baguettes, loaves, and rolls.

PROOFING: This is the final or second rise for the dough before going into the oven. It's a critical step that will determine the lightness of the final product. Underproofing will result in a loaf that has a tight crumb that won't spring much as it bakes and will tear at its seams as if exploding. The overall volume of the loaf will be inadequate. Overproofing or overfermenting, on the other hand, results in dough that is sticky and slack. The dough will overfill with air and, like a balloon, it will "pop" and flatten out completely. A perfectly proofed loaf will feel light in the hand. It will have a beautiful, open, airy crumb, and it will rise gently as it bakes in the oven, opening gracefully where it is scored. New bakers tend to underproof because they are often impatient, so remember this: Baking bread cannot be rushed.

BAKING: Heat transforms dough into bread, and the temperature at which it bakes is of paramount importance, as is the application of steam during this step. Without steam, the bread will form a crust too quickly, and it won't have time to expand in the oven. Steam creates a moist environment so that the loaf can open up fully before browning. I think using a Dutch oven is the best way to create this moist environment, but if you don't have one, you can place a roasting pan full of water on the bottom rack (or floor) of your oven. Underbaked bread will have a doughy interior and a pale crust. The temperature might not have been high enough, or it should have been baked longer. A good, thorough bake at the right temperature will produce a light loaf with deep amber or mahogany color and a beautiful, crisp crust.

COOLING: In most cases, the bread should be allowed to cool for at least 30 minutes before slicing and eating. Cooling sets the crumb and crust. If you try to eat insufficiently cooled bread, it will be difficult to slice, and you'll crush the wet, overly soft crumb. Bread baked in a cast iron Dutch oven or in a loaf pan should be removed and cooled on a wire rack, whereas bread baked on a rimmed baking sheet, like focaccia, can cool on the pan.

Measurements in the Book

Almost all of the ingredients in this book have been measured in grams. This makes it much easier to multiply and divide recipes without making errors, and it's a more accurate form of measurement. Professional bakers use metric weight as the standard. All you need is an inexpensive kitchen scale and you'll be able to weigh all your ingredients in grams quite easily. Once you get accustomed to baking this way, you will never want to fuss with a variety of cups and spoons ever again—it is so much simpler! If you want to halve a recipe, simply divide the numbers of grams in half. Nothing will get lost in fractions here or mixed up while converting back and forth between ounces and pounds. I use rounded-off numbers to make it easy to remember the recipes and to see the ratio of ingredients.

The Many Methods of Creating Bread

There are so many ways to make delicious bread, and now that you have a general overview of how bread is formed, I want to break it down even further and explain the main differences between the most common bread-making methods.

One of the first decisions you must make when baking bread is whether you will use a straight dough or a dough that is created with pre-ferment. If you use a straight dough, your next big decision is whether you want to create a kneaded bread or a no-knead bread. If you choose to make a dough with a pre-ferment, you must decide what type of pre-ferment to make. Below, I will explain what all of this means and what you can expect from each iteration of the bread-making process.

Note that for your ease and education, I've already made the above-mentioned decisions for you and have organized the book accordingly. The recipes in chapters 3, 4, and 5 use straight doughs, while the recipes in chapter 6 teach you how to create and use dough with various pre-ferments.

Poolish, Biga, and
Sourdough Starter
rising in glass jars.

STRAIGHT DOUGHS VERSUS PRE-FERMENTS AND STARTERS

A straight dough—one that doesn't incorporate any pre-ferment or starter—is our starting point for learning how to bake bread. Straight doughs use commercial yeast, and they are mixed beginning to end typically in the same day.

Pre-ferments, on the other hand, use fermentation over time as a way to improve the flavor of the bread. The idea is to incorporate a small bit of pre-fermented dough in with the other bread ingredients, which increases the complexity of flavor. A pre-ferment is a mixture of flour, yeast, and water that is prepared 12 to 18 hours before you plan to mix up the rest of the dough. (Notice that the pre-ferment is made of the same ingredients as the rest of the dough, but the difference is based on what happens to it over time.) A sourdough starter is similar, except that you periodically "feed" more flour and water into it, which keeps it in a constant state of fermentation. Here are three main types of pre-ferments:

POOLISH: Consisting simply of flour, water, and a tiny quantity of yeast, poolish is usually made the day before the bread will be made, and is mixed with cool water so it will have a long, slow rise. Its defining characteristic is that it is a wet, thin mixture—generally a ratio of 1:1 water to flour. Poolish can also impart extensibility to a dough (this is a baker term for "stretchiness"), so it is well suited to pizza dough, focaccia, and baguettes, where those qualities are desired.

BIGA: Following the same concept as poolish, biga combines flour, water, and a small amount of yeast, and is left to ferment. What makes it different from poolish is that it is stiffer because it contains less water. This means that the biga will ferment more slowly than poolish, which means an even longer rise, but the end result will be a more complex flavor. Biga is nice for making loaves that benefit from more structure, like country loaves, breads with whole-grain flour, and ciabatta.

LEVAIN OR SOURDOUGH STARTER: These don't use any commercial yeast. Instead, they rely on yeast that lives on grains and in the air all around us. A starter is a living culture that is cared for continuously by its owner and is typically "fed" each day. There are as many compositions of sourdough as there are bakers in the world and—odd as it may sound—they become a personal reflection of the owner and where he or she lives. Leavening bread with only a living sourdough starter that you make yourself is an art form and creates a truly unique loaf of bread, though it does require lots of practice. We will delve into sourdough at the very end of this book. Once you understand all of the fundamentals of baking less complex breads, you will be ready to tackle sourdough with confidence.

TO KNEAD OR NOT TO KNEAD

Gluten development is a key part of bread baking, and kneading and/or folding the dough is our tool to accomplish that. Both methods develop gluten through friction to create the structure and strength of the dough. The aim is to give the dough the necessary structure to be both strong and cohesive, but not so much so that it is tight and inflexible. The balance between strength and elasticity is important to create beautiful bread. Kneading is best to use for stiffer doughs that need more structure. Folding dough works fine with wetter doughs that would be difficult or frustrating to knead, and it gives a gentler development to the gluten, which is nice for breads with an aerated crumb. Plus, it leaves your dough with elasticity, which is desirable for things like pizza, focaccia, and even baguettes.

No-knead (or folding)

In this book we will start out with folded doughs just to get used to the rhythm of the baking process and all its steps. As you gain confidence, you will move forward to kneaded doughs that will give you an opportunity to practice some more advanced shaping methods.

HOW TO FOLD: Imagine that your dough has four "corners." Pull each corner up and stretch it over the top of the dough to meet the opposite side. Visualizing a clock on the top of your bowl of dough, pull the 12 o'clock corner up and down to 6. Pull the 3 o'clock over to 9, then the 6 o'clock up to 12, and the 9 o'clock over to 3. Work your way around the clock two or three times, until the dough becomes a tight ball and is no longer loose and stretchy.

Kneading

This is a good option when you need more structure in your dough, are working with a loaf that has a slightly lower hydration, and want to have the confidence of shaping a stiffer, stronger dough.

HOW TO KNEAD: Push forward into your dough with the heels of your hands, and then fold the elongated dough back toward you. Give the dough a quarter turn, and then push the dough away and fold it back again. Keep kneading until you can feel that the dough has tightened up and has gotten smoother, usually 5 to 10 minutes. Pop your dough back into the bowl.

Because this book progresses from the easiest recipes to more advanced ones, chapter 3 consists of all no-knead breads, while chapters 4, 5, and 6 contain breads that require kneading.

FOLDING

Stretching and folding the dough over and over builds the strength of the dough.

KNEADING

Kneading, a more thorough approach for creating a strong dough.

Chapter Two

Preparing to Bake

Gathering everything you need for success and going over some basics will empower you to get baking. Here we'll go over the tools of the trade and a few technical things you might need to consider before you make some great loaves of bread. Don't be intimidated by all the equipment—there are many ways to make things work around your kitchen, and the first recipe chapter keeps the equipment needs very basic.

Equipment

You'll need to have just a few pieces of equipment and learn some basic techniques before getting started in your baking practice.

BANNETON OR PROOFING BASKET: For the final proof, the dough needs to be placed in a basket that will allow air to circulate. You can buy baskets specifically for this called bannetons, which are made of cane. If you aren't ready to invest in a couple of bannetons just yet, a round or oval basket from a thrift store can be lined with a floured kitchen towel for a more affordable option. When I first started out, I had a ragtag collection of round and oval-shaped baskets, and they worked just fine.

BOWLS: I love using the large metal mixing bowl that I found at a restaurant supply store, but any bowl will do. Make sure you have a variety of sizes so you can measure out different quantities of ingredients. Whenever I shop at thrift stores, I like finding small bowls for a few cents here and there to add to my collection. Having little bowls for ingredients in smaller amounts, like salt, yeast, chopped herbs, and so on, is nice, but it's not absolutely necessary—any vessel will do.

CAST IRON DUTCH OVEN: This is needed for creating a high-heat, steam-enclosed environment to bake loaves in, and it's the best investment for baking artisan-style loaves in a home oven. You can find these on Amazon for about $35 or at your local kitchen store. Many people already have a cast iron or ceramic Dutch oven in their kitchen, but if you don't, it's well worth the investment. I use a Dutch oven in many of the recipes in the book.

DOUGH SCRAPER: I recommend getting a metal and a plastic dough scraper. They cost just a few dollars at kitchen stores, at restaurant supply stores, or on Amazon, and they are so useful. A metal scraper is helpful for cutting and scraping dough off your work area, and a plastic scraper is flexible enough to help scrape the dough out of the bowl after rising.

KITCHEN SCALE: Almost all of the ingredients in the recipes are measured in grams, so you will need a kitchen scale that weighs in metrics. Weighing your ingredients is the best way to get the most consistent results in your baking, and once you get used to weighing your ingredients, I promise you won't want to go back. It is so much simpler and makes a huge difference in the final loaf of bread. Kitchen scales are relatively inexpensive these days; small ones can be found for around $20. They typically have a "mode" button that will easily switch them from ounces to grams.

LOAF PANS: I recommend buying two 9-by-5-by-3-inch rectangular loaf pans, which is probably the most common size found at stores. My favorite pan is from USA Pan, and it can be found online. The loaves never ever stick to them. I use a 9-by-5-by-3-inch loaf pan for all of the loaf-style breads in this book.

NOTEBOOK AND PEN: I can't say enough that when you are starting out, different baking results will occur and you will want to know why you got those results. The only way to find out is to record what you did. Think of it like running a series of scientific experiments. Everything being equal, knowing what variables have changed and what haven't can lead you to where you went right or wrong.

PEEL: This is a flat wooden board with a handle for loading bread or pizza onto a baking stone in the oven. If you don't have one, it's no problem—I used a thin wooden cutting board for years, and it is a fine option.

PIZZA STONE OR BAKING STONE: These are preheated in the oven and help build the perfect crust while baking bread and pizza. If you don't have one, you can bake on an inverted baking sheet lined with parchment, but the results won't be quite the same.

RAZOR BLADE OR LAME: A razor blade is the best tool for slashing the top of a loaf of bread. A lame is a tool that holds the razor blade safely and has a nice handle, which makes it even easier to make precision slashes. My favorite lame is made by Mure & Peyrot and can be found on Amazon for only $15. You won't need one for the first chapter of this book, but you will as you move on to more advanced recipes.

RIMMED BAKING SHEET: This is an item you likely have in your kitchen already, and if not, it's a worthwhile investment. I usually use a 12-by-18-inch or a 16-by-24-inch baking sheet, which can be found at restaurant supply stores and online. In some recipes within this book, I call for a 16-by-24-inch baking sheet, but if a 12-by-18-inch sheet fits better in your oven, feel free to substitute it in.

THERMOMETER: To achieve consistency in your baking, you'll need to know the temperature of your water and the ingredients. Buy a probe thermometer to check temperatures of ingredients. I also recommend you have an oven thermometer to be sure the temperature of your oven is accurate. You can purchase these for around $20 on Amazon and in most grocery stores.

Other items you may need that are usually part of any kitchen:

- Kitchen towels
- Nonstick cooking spray
- Parchment paper
- Pastry brush
- Plastic wrap
- Scissors
- Spray bottle
- Rubber spatula

A lame keeps fingers safe and makes it much easier to get creative when scoring.

What to Know before You Start

To get the best possible results, think of the process of baking bread as a science. If you learn the basic balance of ingredients, hydration, and temperature shown here, you'll get a great loaf of bread.

MEASURE IN WEIGHT.

I weigh all my ingredients. It's more accurate than volume measurements, and it's easier to measure small amounts. The best thing? No need to use all those measuring cups and spoons. All you need is a bowl and your scale.

TEMPERATURE IS KEY.

WATER TEMPERATURE: Water temperature is such a vital factor in bread baking, it should be considered one of the ingredients. The temperature of the water is what ultimately creates the temperature of the dough, and that determines how long the dough will take to rise. Guessing the temperature of water won't work. Warm water can vary by as much as 40 degrees, a huge variance in bread baking. Yeasted breads ferment best at a temperature between 75°F and 78°F.

AIR TEMPERATURE: Room temperature in your house will likely vary throughout the year, and this temperature is another important factor in fermentation. When it's very cold in the winter, you'll need to use a higher water temperature to ensure the correct final dough temperature. In summertime, the opposite case will be true. Consistent bread baking through the seasons can be accomplished with a bit of mindfulness and calculation. You'll be surprised by how much temperatures can vary from day to day once you start taking note of it. One simple way to estimate the temperature of your home is to take the temperature of your flour while it is sitting out in the kitchen.

TIME IS AN INGREDIENT.

If I'm going to consider temperature an ingredient in baking, then so, too, is time. Time is the overall key to unlocking the flavor in bread. The same ingredients can have wildly varying results if only the variables of time and temperature are changed, and the management of these two ingredients is what ultimately determines the end result. As a general rule, the length of time of fermentation and the overall flavor of the final loaf are related. The timing of any pre-ferments, the timing of the bulk fermentation as related to temperature, the resting time for the dough, the time to proof the dough, and, yes, even the time in the oven all need to be correct—and are all vital ingredients—for success.

Temperature Calculation

Use this example to find your desired water temperature.

**Take the desired
dough temperature:**
75°F

Multiply that number by 3:
75 × 3 = 225

(This is because there are three factors: flour temperature, air temperature, and water temperature.)

Determine the temperature of the flour and the air:

Flour temperature: 65°F
Air temperature: 65°F
Friction factor: 5

(This number will always be 5 for hand-mixed doughs, which are used in this book.)

**Take 225 and subtract
the other factors to arrive at
the desired water temperature:**
225 − (65 + 65 + 5) = 90,
meaning you will use
90°F water on this day.

The dough should always be 75°F or above, so 225 will always be the number for the overall dough temperature factor, and the friction factor will always be 5, so it's easy to take the temperature of flour and air and then calculate to get the desired water temperature. Usually, the air and flour will be the same temperature, but sometimes they can vary, which is why I suggest checking both temperatures before doing your calculations.

I know that doing math before baking seems like a lot, but when you invest the ingredients, time, and effort into creating something wonderful, those 2 minutes of calculations are truly worth the effort!

You can use this chart as a shortcut, assuming that your flour and air temperatures are the same. Making your own calculations is more accurate, but this is a good starting place.

Air and flour temperature	Water temperature
55	110
60	100
65	90
70	80
75	70
80	60
85	50

Notice how much the indoor temperature of your home varies between winter and summer. You'll need to adjust the water temperature to ensure proper fermentation throughout the year. When it gets very hot here in California in the summer, I add ice to the mixing water to keep temperatures down. Imagine disregarding temperatures and mixing with water from the hot side of the tap (which can be 120°F in the summer). The effects can be drastic, and not in a good way!

Your starting point will be a simple straight dough that comes together in an afternoon. As you learn and practice, you will stretch out that fermentation time, acquire new skills, and push toward incorporating pre-ferments and prolonging the final proof. These are all building blocks for great, flavorful loaves of bread, and once you have the skills and knowledge, your investment of that extra time will pay off in the final result.

How Altitude Affects Baking

High-altitude environments have lower air pressure and can also suffer from less moisture in the air, which can make yeasted bread rise too quickly, be too dry, and bake more quickly. A few changes that can be made to accommodate a high-altitude environment:

- Reducing the quantity of yeast by one-quarter, slightly increasing the amount of water as necessary

- Using a slightly cooler water temperature than called for to slow the rise

- Slightly lowering the oven temperature to prevent overbaking

Use these adjustments as a starting point. However, it is likely that you will need to tinker with your recipe and tailor it to your specific environment.

- prep dough
- proof dough

- leaven mix /
  reload starter
- cookie dough
- salt / seeds
- brioche scale / as
- butter block
- lock in ✓
- fold dough ✓

- eat lunch /
  cook for kids
- invert + test cream

PART TWO

RECIPES

Chapter Three

No-Knead Breads

Rustic Loaves, Focaccias, Pizza, and Fougasse

This chapter is a gentle introduction to bread baking for the beginner, and these are the types of recipes I learned first when I started baking my own bread. You'll begin by focusing on doing the basic tasks of creating a loaf and getting the general feel of how a bread-baking practice can be folded into the fabric of your life without too much fuss. You'll start with a simple, rustic loaf and then you'll see how you can take that dough to make focaccia or fougasse (a beautiful, leaf-shaped bread). You'll also make your own pizza! I love starting here with new bakers because these recipes are a wonderful, minimalist way to get acquainted with the basic needs of good bread: a full fermentation and a great proof. Let's start making some bread!

No-Knead Bread

This recipe will provide you with the simplest, most basic way to get a loaf of bread onto your table. Remember that while all of the necessary instructions are here to make a great loaf of bread, a small part of baking will be the development of your intuition, senses, judgment, and skills, which are all built by practice. If you feel your very first loaf isn't a slam dunk, check through the Common Problems and FAQs at the end of the recipe to determine how to improve next time. Then try again!

MAKES 1 LOAF

PREP TIME: 15 minutes (5 minutes to mix the dough, 5 minutes to fold the dough, and 5 minutes to shape the dough)

INACTIVE TIME: 20 minutes to rest, 1 hour 30 minutes to rise, 1 hour to 1 hour 30 minutes to proof the dough and preheat the oven

BAKE TIME: 40 to 45 minutes

TOOLS NEEDED: thermometer, kitchen scale, large bowl, round basket, kitchen towel, Dutch oven

8 grams instant yeast
375 grams water
500 grams all-purpose flour
10 grams salt

1. PREPARE: Find the ambient temperature of your kitchen with a thermometer. A great way to do this is to take the temperature of your flour while it is sitting out at room temperature. Take a look at the chart on page 21 to see what temperature water you need for your dough. I find the easiest way to get my water to the correct temperature is to fill a pitcher or jar with hot water and one with cold water from the tap. I pour the cold water into the hot water until I've reached the ideal temperature. The desired dough temperature here is 76°F.

2. SCALE: Weigh all of the ingredients separately before you begin. This helps keep everything accurate. Use smaller bowls for ingredients in smaller amounts, like yeast and salt, to get the most precise reading.

CONTINUED →

3. COMBINE: In a large bowl, disperse the yeast into the water with a gentle swish of your fingers, like making a bubble bath. Let it sit for a couple of minutes. You should see a light foaming from the yeast, letting you know that it is feeling lively and ready to go to work for you. Next, add the flour on top of the water and yeast. Last, sprinkle the salt on top of the flour. This keeps it from coming into direct contact with the yeast, which can inhibit the rise.

4. MIX: I like to use my hands. If you have an aversion to getting a bit sticky, a nice, sturdy wooden spoon can do the trick on this wetter dough. I think hand mixing is really helpful for feeling that the ingredients are well combined. The ingredients should come together easily and produce a slack, wet dough.

5. REST: Let your dough relax for about 20 minutes so the flour can absorb the water a bit. Make yourself a cup of tea, my friend.

6. FOLD: Stretch and fold the dough, which will give it strength so it can hold its shape in the oven later. Imagine that your dough has four "corners." Pull each corner up and stretch it over the top of the dough to meet the opposite side. Visualizing a clock on the top of your bowl of dough, pull the 12 o'clock corner up and down to 6. Pull the 3 o'clock over to 9, then the 6 o'clock up to 12, and the 9 o'clock over to 3. Work your way around the clock two or three times, until the dough becomes a tight ball and is no longer loose and

stretchy. You have just achieved some gluten development! Wasn't that easy?

7. RISE: Place a floured kitchen towel (or plastic wrap if that's what you have) over your bowl, and go enjoy your life for 1 hour 30 minutes. Definitely don't stare at your dough the whole time—your dough will do its own thing until you come back to it.

8. CHECK: At 1 hour 30 minutes, the dough should be noticeably lighter, larger, and filled with air bubbles. To double-check, fill a cup with water, pinch off a little ball of your dough, and drop it into the glass. It should float to the top, indicating that your dough is aerated. Nice! If it doesn't seem particularly buoyant, it might be a cold day at your house. No worries. Let it rise a bit longer and check it again in 30 minutes or so.

9. SHAPE: Gently turn your dough onto a floured countertop. The bottom, which was in contact with the bowl, will be facing up to you. If it is sticking to the bowl, use your hand or a plastic scraper to release it. Shape this dough easily by giving it a gentle letter fold: Fold the far side (12 o'clock) down to the middle, sealing the dough against itself. Now fold the bottom up to meet the seam and seal it. Turn the dough so this seam is vertical, and do that letter fold again, sealing the dough to itself. You should have a nice little rounded square shape. If the dough

CONTINUED ➔

Folding, a simple technique for creating strength and tension in the dough.

is nice and tight, you can stop there. If it seems very relaxed, you can give it another set of letter folds to create more tension, sealing the dough to itself.

10. PROOF: Place your dough round into a basket lined with a floured kitchen towel, seam-side down. You are going to let this dough rise for 1 hour to 1 hour 30 minutes, until the dough feels airy, like a marshmallow. When pressed with a finger, it should leave an indent instead of springing back up. This is the final rise before it hops into the oven.

11. PREHEAT: While the dough is proofing, turn on your oven with an empty Dutch oven inside and let it preheat to 475°F. This may seem early to preheat the oven, but great bread needs a thoroughly hot oven for the best results.

12. CHECK: To test that the dough is well proofed, press a finger gently into the dough. If it seems springy and tight, it needs more time. If it feels airy and light (like a marshmallow), it's ready to bake. Needing more time for proofing is a common theme in baking bread. Don't let it worry you if your dough needs more time to rise! Feeling the dough and adapting to the timing needs every time you bake bread is the way to become a better baker, so let your senses guide you.

13. BAKE: Flour your work surface well and tip the loaf out of your basket onto it, seam-side up. Carefully pull your very hot Dutch oven out of the oven and place it on top of the stove with the lid next to it. Pick the dough up with your hands and gently drop it into the Dutch oven, seam-side up (it will open at that seam, resulting in a classic rustic loaf), and be careful to avoid burning your hands. (Don't worry about scoring this loaf with a knife or razor blade; we will practice that in chapter 4, with kneaded loaves.) Cover the Dutch oven with the lid, slide it into the oven, and bake for 25 minutes.

14. CHECK: At 25 minutes, take the cover off the Dutch oven. You should see a pale blond loaf that has risen to meet you. Continue baking with the cover removed for another 15 to 20 minutes. Your loaf will get some color and develop a nice crust. The finished loaf should be golden brown and will sound hollow when you thump it with your fingers. If the loaf seems to be browning too quickly, turn your oven down to 450°F.

15. COOL: Let your finished loaf cool on a wire rack for 30 minutes to let the interior crumb set, making it easier to slice. You've just made your first loaf of bread!

Common Problems and FAQs

Q: Why was my loaf dense and not full of air bubbles?

A: Often this is a timing or temperature issue. Make sure that your water temperature is warm enough, that you are checking for air in your dough after it rises and proofs, and that you are checking for a successful final proof.

Q: Why did my loaf deflate when I put it in the oven and come out flat?

A: This is an overproofing issue. Check that your water and dough temperatures are correct and not too hot, and make sure that you don't let your final proof go too long.

Q: Why was my loaf very slack and difficult to shape?

A: This is an underdevelopment or overhydration issue. Be sure to give your dough adequate folds when shaping so it will keep its structure in the oven. Weigh your ingredients, which will ensure your dough isn't too wet or too dry. The other possibility is that you are using a very-low-gluten flour. Try again using a bread flour or King Arthur unbleached all-purpose flour, which is higher in protein than other brands. Alternatively, hold back 20 to 40 grams of the water to produce a dough that is easier to handle.

Q: Why is my bread pale and not browning nicely?

A: This is an overfermentation issue. When your bread ferments, the yeast eats up the sugars in the dough. If there are no sugars left due to overfermentation, you won't have enough of the necessary sugars to caramelize into a lovely crust. Check that your water and dough temperatures aren't too hot, and try not to leave your dough in a very hot location (like near a hot stove).

Q: My loaf burned on the bottom before it browned on the top. How can I change this?

A: Your heating element may be on the bottom of the oven. You can move the Dutch oven up to a higher rack in the oven and slide a pan onto the rack below it to protect the bottom of your bread.

Q: My loaf didn't turn out good at all. What can I do with it?

A: You can always make bread crumbs by cutting up your loaf and running it through a food processor!

8-Hour Fermentation No-Knead Bread

This variation of the basic no-knead formula adjusts the quantity of yeast for a longer rise time. It's a great way to make a loaf of bread when you work an 8-hour day. You can mix and fold the dough in the morning and come home, bake the dough, and have bread with dinner. You can use this variation for all of the other recipes in this chapter, as well. The longer rise time also gives your loaf a wonderful flavor, so even if you don't work outside the home but have a long day ahead of you, this is a great option.

MAKES 1 LOAF

PREP TIME: 15 minutes (5 minutes to mix the dough, 5 minutes to fold the dough, and 5 minutes to shape the dough)

INACTIVE TIME: 20 minutes to rest, 8 hours to rise, 1 hour to 1 hour 30 minutes to proof the dough and preheat the oven

BAKE TIME: 40 to 45 minutes

TOOLS NEEDED: thermometer, kitchen scale, large bowl, round basket, kitchen towel, Dutch oven

3 grams instant yeast
375 grams water
500 grams all-purpose flour
10 grams salt

1. CREATE THE DOUGH: Follow the Master Recipe for No-Knead Bread (page 28) through step 6, using the ingredient amounts listed.

2. RISE: Place a floured kitchen towel (or plastic wrap if that's what you have) over your bowl, and go enjoy your life for 8 hours.

3. CHECK: At 8 hours, the dough should be noticeably lighter, larger, and filled with air bubbles. To double-check, fill a cup with water, pinch off a little ball of your dough, and drop it into the glass. It should float to the top, indicating that your dough is aerated. Nice! If it doesn't seem particularly buoyant, it might be a cold day at your house. No worries. Let it rise a bit longer and check it again in 30 minutes or so.

4. SHAPE: Gently turn your dough onto a floured countertop. The bottom, which was in contact with the bowl, will be facing up to you. If it is sticking to the bowl, use your hand or a plastic scraper to release it. Shape this dough easily by giving it a gentle letter fold: Fold the far side (12 o'clock) down to the middle, sealing the dough against itself. Now fold the bottom up to meet the seam and seal it. Turn the dough so this seam is vertical, and do that letter fold again, sealing the dough to itself. You should have a nice little rounded square shape. If the dough is nice and tight, you can stop there. If it seems very relaxed, you can give it another set of letter folds to create more tension, sealing the dough to itself.

5. PROOF: Place your dough round into a basket lined with a floured kitchen towel, seam-side down. You are going to let this dough rise for 1 hour to 1 hour 30 minutes, until the dough feels airy, like a marshmallow. When pressed with a finger, it should leave an indent instead of springing back up. This is the final rise before it hops into the oven.

6. PREHEAT: While the dough is proofing, turn on your oven with an empty Dutch oven inside and let it preheat to 475°F. This may seem early to preheat the oven, but great bread needs a thoroughly hot oven for the best results.

7. CHECK: To test that the dough is well proofed, press a finger gently into the dough. If it seems springy and tight, it needs more time. If it feels airy and light (like a marshmallow), it's ready to bake. Needing more time for proofing is a common theme in baking bread. Don't let it worry you if your dough needs more time to rise! Feeling the dough and adapting to the timing needs every time you bake bread is the way to become a better baker, so let your senses guide you.

8. BAKE: Flour your work surface well and tip the loaf out of your basket onto it, seam-side up. Carefully pull your very hot Dutch oven out of the oven and place it on top of the stove with the lid next to it. Pick the dough up with your hands and gently drop it into the Dutch oven, seam-side up (it will open at that seam, resulting in a classic rustic loaf), and be careful to avoid burning your hands. (Don't worry about scoring this loaf with a knife or razor blade; we will practice that in chapter 4, with kneaded loaves.) Cover the Dutch oven with the lid, slide it into the oven, and bake for 25 minutes.

9. CHECK: At 25 minutes, take the cover off the Dutch oven. You should see a pale blond loaf that has risen to meet you. Continue baking with the cover removed for another 15 to 20 minutes. Your loaf will get some color and develop a nice crust. The finished loaf should be golden brown and will sound hollow when you thump it with your fingers. If the loaf seems to be browning too quickly, turn your oven down to 450°F.

10. COOL: Let your finished loaf cool on a wire rack for 30 minutes to let the interior crumb set, making it easier to slice.

12-Hour Fermentation No-Knead Bread

This variation of the no-knead formula adjusts the quantity of yeast for an even longer rise time. It's a great way to make a loaf of bread on the weekend. You can mix and fold the dough in the evening, then wake up to shape and bake. You can use this variation for all of the other recipes in this chapter, as well. The even longer rise time also gives your loaf a wonderful flavor.

MAKES 1 LOAF

PREP TIME: 15 minutes (5 minutes to mix the dough, 5 minutes to fold the dough, and 5 minutes to shape the dough)

INACTIVE TIME: 20 minutes to rest, 12 hours to rise, 1 to 1 hour 30 minutes to proof the dough and preheat the oven

BAKE TIME: 40 to 45 minutes

TOOLS NEEDED: thermometer, kitchen scale, large bowl, round basket, kitchen towel, Dutch oven

1 gram instant yeast
375 grams water
500 grams all-purpose flour
10 grams salt

1. CREATE THE DOUGH: Follow the Master Recipe for No-Knead Bread (page 28) through step 6, using the ingredient amounts listed.

2. RISE: Place a floured kitchen towel (or plastic wrap if that's what you have) over your bowl, and go enjoy your life for 12 hours.

3. CHECK: At 12 hours, the dough should be noticeably lighter, larger, and filled with air bubbles. To double-check, fill a cup with water, pinch off a little ball of your dough, and drop it into the glass. It should float to the top, indicating that your dough is aerated. Nice! If it doesn't seem particularly buoyant, it might be a cold day at your house. No worries. Let it rise a bit longer and check it again in 30 minutes or so.

4. SHAPE: Gently turn your dough onto a floured countertop. The bottom, which was in contact with the bowl, will be facing up to you. If it is sticking to the bowl, use your hand or a plastic scraper to release it. Shape this dough easily by giving it a gentle letter fold: Fold the far side (12 o'clock) down to the middle, sealing the dough against itself. Now fold the bottom up to meet the seam and seal it. Turn the dough so this seam is vertical, and do that letter fold again, sealing the dough to itself. You should have a nice little rounded square shape. If the dough is nice and tight, you can stop there. If it seems very relaxed, you can give it another set of letter folds to create more tension, sealing the dough to itself.

5. PROOF: Place your dough round into a basket lined with a floured kitchen towel, seam-side down. You are going to let this dough rise for 1 hour to 1 hour 30 minutes, until the dough feels airy, like a marshmallow. When pressed with a finger, it should leave an indent instead of springing back up. This is the final rise before it hops into the oven.

6. PREHEAT: While the dough is proofing, turn on your oven with an empty Dutch oven inside and let it preheat to 475°F. This may seem early to preheat the oven, but great bread needs a thoroughly hot oven for the best results.

7. CHECK: To test that the dough is well proofed, press a finger gently into the dough. If it seems springy and tight, it needs more time. If it feels airy and light (like a marshmallow), it's ready to bake. Needing more time for proofing is a common theme in baking bread. Don't let it worry you if your dough needs more time to rise! Feeling the dough and adapting to the timing needs every time you bake bread is the way to become a better baker, so let your senses guide you.

8. BAKE: Flour your work surface well and tip the loaf out of your basket onto it, seam-side up. Carefully pull your very hot Dutch oven out of the oven and place it on top of the stove with the lid next to it. Pick the dough up with your hands and gently drop it into the Dutch oven, seam-side up (it will open at that seam, resulting in a classic rustic loaf), and be careful to avoid burning your hands. (Don't worry about scoring this loaf with a knife or razor blade; we will practice that in chapter 4, with kneaded loaves.) Cover the Dutch oven with the lid, slide it into the oven, and bake for 25 minutes.

9. CHECK: At 25 minutes, take the cover off the Dutch oven. You should see a pale blond loaf that has risen to meet you. Continue baking with the cover removed for another 15 to 20 minutes. Your loaf will get some color and develop a nice crust. The finished loaf should be golden brown and will sound hollow when you thump it with your fingers. If the loaf seems to be browning too quickly, turn your oven down to 450°F.

10.COOL: Let your finished loaf cool on a wire rack for 30 minutes to let the interior crumb set, making it easier to slice.

Panned Loaf

Baking a loaf in a pan is a great way to make bread without fussing around with a Dutch oven or other steaming methods. I like making a loaf like this for sandwiches for my kids, since the slices all end up being the same size, unlike more rustic loaf shapes. If you need to fill a lunchbox for yourself or someone else, this is the bread to choose.

MAKES 1 LOAF

PREP TIME: 15 minutes (5 minutes to mix the dough, 5 minutes to fold the dough, and 5 minutes to shape the dough)

INACTIVE TIME: 20 minutes to rest, 1 hour 30 minutes to rise, 1 hour to 1 hour 30 minutes to proof the dough and preheat the oven

BAKE TIME: 45 minutes

TOOLS NEEDED: thermometer, kitchen scale, large bowl, kitchen towel, 9-by-5-by-3-inch loaf pan, pastry brush

FOR THE DOUGH
8 grams instant yeast
370 grams water
500 grams all-purpose flour
10 grams salt
Butter, oil, or cooking spray, for
    greasing the pan

FOR THE EGG WASH (OPTIONAL)
1 egg
2 tablespoons milk

1. CREATE THE DOUGH: Follow the Master Recipe for No-Knead Bread (page 28) through step 8, using the ingredient amounts listed.

2. SHAPE: Gently turn your dough onto a floured countertop. The bottom, which was in contact with the bowl, will be facing up to you. If it is sticking to the bowl, use your hand or a plastic scraper to release it. Shape this dough easily by giving it a gentle letter fold: Fold the far side (12 o'clock) down to the middle, sealing the dough against itself. Now fold the bottom up to meet the seam and seal it. Turn the dough so this seam is vertical, and do that letter fold again, sealing the dough to itself. You should have a nice little rounded square shape. If the dough is nice and tight, you can stop there. If it seems very relaxed, you can give it another set of letter folds to create more tension, sealing the dough to itself.

3. PROOF: Gently place the dough in a greased loaf pan, seam-side down. Proof until the dough starts to crest or "mushroom" up out of the top of the pan, about 1 hour 30 minutes.

4. PREHEAT: While the dough is proofing, preheat the oven to 375°F. Place your oven rack on the bottom level of the oven.

5. BRUSH: After the dough is proofed, if using the egg wash, whisk the egg with the milk in a bowl and brush the mixture onto the top of the loaf before baking. If you are not using the egg wash, brush the top of the loaf generously with water to keep the loaf from forming a hard top.

6. BAKE: Bake the loaf for 45 minutes. At 20 minutes, check the oven to make sure the top of the loaf isn't browning too quickly. If it is, you can protect it by tenting foil over the top of the loaf. The finished loaf should be golden brown and will sound hollow when you thump it with your fingers.

7. COOL: Remove your loaf from the pan right after taking it out of the oven and let cool on a wire rack for at least 30 minutes before slicing. If you leave the bread in the pan to cool, the crust will steam and get soggy, and the loaf will be difficult to remove from the pan.

No-Knead Simple Focaccia

It's fun to cut this large sheet of bread into smaller squares—an easy way to make a lot of snacks for a crowd when you're having people over. Plus it takes wonderfully to being scattered with fresh herbs if you feel creative. To do so, sprinkle a couple of tablespoons of your favorite herbs over the dough just before baking.

MAKES 1 FOCACCIA

PREP TIME: 15 minutes (5 minutes to mix the dough, 5 minutes to fold the dough, and 5 minutes to shape the dough)

INACTIVE TIME: 20 minutes to rest, 1 hour 30 minutes to rise, 30 to 40 minutes for the dough to rest and preheat the oven

BAKE TIME: 20 to 25 minutes

TOOLS NEEDED: thermometer, kitchen scale, large bowl, round basket, kitchen towel, 16-by-24-inch rimmed baking sheet, roasting pan

FOR THE DOUGH
8 grams instant yeast
375 grams water
500 grams all-purpose flour
10 grams salt
Oil, for greasing the pan

FOR THE FOCACCIA TOPPING
¼ cup olive oil
2 tablespoons flaky sea salt

CONTINUED →

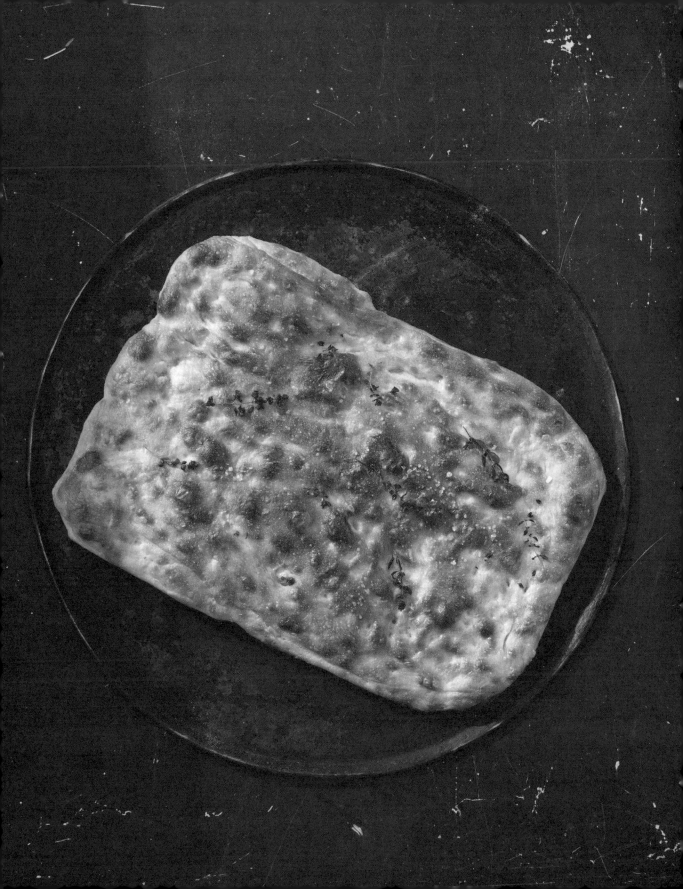

1. CREATE THE DOUGH: Follow the Master Recipe for No-Knead Bread (page 28) through step 8.

2. SHAPE: Oil a 16-by-24-inch rimmed baking sheet. Pull your dough out of the bowl and drop it directly onto the sheet. Pour the olive oil over the dough and start gently stretching the dough toward the four corners of the pan. Using your fingertips, dimple the top of the dough, but be gentle—you don't want to press all of the air bubbles out of your dough. Sprinkle the sea salt over the top of the dough.

3. PREHEAT: Let the dough rest in the pan and preheat the oven to 475°F. Set one oven rack in the center position and one in the lowest position. Don't worry if your dough starts to shrink back after being stretched. The dough will relax if you give it time.

4. BAKE: Focaccia needs a bit of steam for the first few minutes of baking to help it rise. To accomplish this without a Dutch oven, place a roasting pan on the bottom rack of the oven and let it preheat. Pour hot water into the roasting pan until it's about 1 inch deep. This will create steam. Slide the baking sheet with the dough onto the center rack. Bake with steam for 10 minutes. Then take the roasting pan of water out of the oven. Let any remaining steam out of the oven. Bake for 10 to 15 more minutes, until the focaccia is golden brown.

5. COOL: Let cool on the baking sheet for 20 minutes before cutting into squares and serving.

Focaccia with Parmesan, Figs, and Walnuts

This is a wonderful focaccia for sharing with friends, especially with a glass of wine on the porch on a late summer evening. I would put this out with a simple, dressed green salad alongside it. Having a friend with a fig tree that you can climb, like we do, definitely helps with this recipe, but you can substitute other soft fruits available in your region, like nectarines or peaches. I like to pair it with my favorite cheese. Drizzling with a bit of honey at the end is also fun, so feel free to be creative here!

MAKES 1 FOCACCIA

PREP TIME: 15 minutes (5 minutes to mix the dough, 5 minutes to fold the dough, and 5 minutes to shape the dough)

INACTIVE TIME: 20 minutes to rest, 1 hour 30 minutes to rise, 30 to 40 minutes for the dough to rest and preheat the oven

BAKE TIME: 20 to 25 minutes

TOOLS NEEDED: thermometer, kitchen scale, large bowl, kitchen towel, 16-by-24-inch rimmed baking sheet, roasting pan

FOR THE DOUGH
8 grams instant yeast
375 grams water
500 grams all-purpose flour
10 grams salt
Oil, for greasing the pan

FOR THE FOCACCIA TOPPING
¼ cup olive oil, divided
2 tablespoons flaky sea salt
½ cup figs (fresh or dried), roughly chopped
¼ cup walnuts
½ cup shaved Parmesan cheese
Cracked black pepper (optional)

CONTINUED ➔

1. CREATE THE DOUGH: Follow the Master Recipe for No-Knead Bread (page 28) through step 8.

2. SHAPE: Oil a 16-by-24-inch rimmed baking sheet. Pull your dough out of the bowl and drop it directly onto the sheet. Pour half of the olive oil over the dough and start gently stretching the dough toward the four corners of the pan. Using your fingertips, dimple the top of the dough, but be gentle—you don't want to press all of the air bubbles out of your dough. Sprinkle the sea salt over the top of the dough with your fingers.

3. PREHEAT: Let the dough rest in the pan and preheat the oven to 475°F. Set one oven rack in the center position and one in the lowest position. Don't worry if your dough starts to shrink back after being stretched. The dough will relax if you give it time.

4. MIX: In a bowl, toss the figs and walnuts together in the remaining olive oil. Just before baking, scatter this mixture and the shaved Parmesan all over the focaccia dough.

5. BAKE: Focaccia needs a bit of steam for the first few minutes of baking to help it rise. To accomplish this without a Dutch oven, place a roasting pan on the bottom rack of the oven and let it preheat. Pour hot water into the roasting pan until it's about 1 inch deep. This will create steam. Slide the baking sheet with the dough onto the center rack. Bake with steam for 10 minutes. Then take the roasting pan of water out of the oven. Let any remaining steam out of the oven. Bake for 10 to 15 more minutes, until the focaccia is golden brown.

6. COOL: Let cool on a wire rack for 15 minutes before cutting into squares. Shave more Parmesan over the focaccia and top with cracked black pepper, if using, before serving.

Ficelles
(Simple Rustic Baguettes)

These little rustic baguettes make a wonderful canvas for sandwiches. With a soft, airy interior and crisp crust, they are perfect for making savory goods wrapped for picnics, and it's as simple as cutting a focaccia into long strips.

MAKES 4 TO 6 FICELLES

PREP TIME: 15 minutes (5 minutes to mix the dough, 5 minutes to fold the dough, and 5 minutes to divide and shape the dough)

INACTIVE TIME: 20 minutes to rest, 1 hour 30 minutes to rise, 30 to 45 minutes to proof the dough and preheat the oven

BAKE TIME: 20 to 25 minutes

TOOLS NEEDED: thermometer, kitchen scale, large bowl, kitchen towel, 16-by-24-inch rimmed baking sheet, pizza cutter or sharp knife

FOR THE DOUGH
8 grams instant yeast
375 grams water
500 grams all-purpose flour
10 grams salt
Oil, for greasing the pan

FOR THE FICELLE TOPPING
¼ cup olive oil

1. CREATE THE DOUGH: Follow the Master Recipe for No-Knead Bread (page 28) through step 8.

2. SHAPE: Oil a 16-by-24-inch rimmed baking sheet. Pull your dough out of the bowl and drop it directly onto the sheet. Press the dough gently into a rough rectangle. Using a pizza cutter or a sharp knife, cut the dough into 4 to 6 equal pieces. Pour the olive oil over the dough pieces and gently stretch each strip into an elongated baguette shape. Don't worry if they have a bit of character to them.

3. PROOF: Let the ficelles proof for 30 to 45 minutes, until they are puffy and airy and feel like a marshmallow. When pressed with a finger, it should leave an indent instead of springing back up.

4. PREHEAT: While the dough is proofing, preheat the oven to 475°F and set the rack in the middle position of the oven.

5. BAKE: Bake for 20 to 25 minutes, until the ficelles are light golden brown.

6. COOL: Let cool on a wire rack for at least 30 minutes to let the interior crumb set and make it easier to slice.

Pizza with Tomato and Mozzarella

This simple pizza is a great way to get dinner on the table and please everyone. We have pizza every Saturday afternoon, and the whole family looks forward to it. I used to try to think of new and creative toppings for our pizzas, but we have settled on tomatoes, mozzarella, and basil—often called a Margherita pizza—as our favorite.

MAKES 2 PIZZAS

PREP TIME: 15 minutes (5 minutes to mix the dough, 5 minutes to fold the dough, and 5 minutes to divide and shape the dough)

INACTIVE TIME: 20 minutes to rest, 1 hour 30 minutes to rise, 30 minutes for the dough to rest and preheat the oven

BAKE TIME: 9 to 18 minutes

TOOLS NEEDED: thermometer, kitchen scale, large bowl, kitchen towel, baking stone or baking sheet, peel or wooden cutting board

FOR THE DOUGH
8 grams instant yeast
375 grams water
500 grams all-purpose flour
10 grams salt

FOR THE PIZZA TOPPING
¼ cup olive oil
1 (16-ounce) can crushed tomatoes
16 ounces fresh mozzarella
Fresh basil
Red pepper flakes
Additional toppings of your choice

CONTINUED →

Shaping and topping the pizza dough.

1. CREATE THE DOUGH: Follow the Master Recipe for No-Knead Bread (page 28) through step 8.

2. PRESHAPE: Divide the dough into 2 equal pieces and form each into a ball. Press each piece of dough into flat rounds by pressing it with your hands against the work surface. Dust the dough with flour, cover with a kitchen towel, and let the dough relax for at least 30 minutes.

3. PREHEAT: While the dough is relaxing, preheat your oven to at least 450°F or at the highest possible temperature. Set the rack at the lowest position in the oven. Place your baking stone on the oven rack. (If you don't have a baking

stone, invert a baking sheet, cover with parchment, and preheat it in the oven. After stretching the dough, place it on the parchment, add toppings, and slide it onto the hot pan in the oven.) This may seem like a long time to preheat an oven, but great pizza needs a thoroughly hot oven for success.

4. SHAPE: Sprinkle a generous amount of flour on your pizza peel or wooden cutting board and place the dough on top. The flour will keep the dough from sticking to the peel when you try to slide it onto the hot baking stone. (My other tip to avoid sticking is to move the assembled

CONTINUED →

pizza from the peel to the oven as soon as possible.) Flour one of the dough rounds and gently press it down onto the peel so you have a flattish circle. Now take your fingers and dimple around the edge of your circle to give it a rim of definition of where the crust will be. Stretch the dough carefully by resting it over your fist, letting gravity help it stretch. Switch hands and turn the dough until it has stretched to the size you would like. Be gentle and avoid stretching the dough too thin in the center.

5. TOP: Drizzle the olive oil around the crust of the pizza. Spread a light layer of crushed tomatoes over the dough, leaving the crust area bare. Tear pieces of fresh mozzarella and arrange them around the dough. Scatter a handful of fresh basil leaves over the cheese and finish with a sprinkling of red pepper flakes.

6. SLIDE: Give your peel a little shake to make sure that your pizza is not sticking to the peel and will slide. (Trust me, shooting a bunch of cheese into the back of your oven while the dough crumples attached to your peel can be funny, but it's no fun to clean up.) If the dough seems sticky, use a dough scraper to pull up the dough and scatter more flour under the pizza to help it along. Put your peel into the oven, aligning the far edge of the pizza with the far side of the pizza stone. Give the peel a gentle nudge to help the far edge of the pizza start to slide onto the stone. Once it's in position, give your peel a brisk pull, and your pizza will slide fully onto the pizza stone.

7. BAKE: Bake for anywhere from 9 to 18 minutes. Oven temperatures can vary widely, so keep an eye on your pizza the first few times you bake to figure out the best baking time for you. Repeat to shape, top, slide, and bake the second pizza.

8. SERVE: Cut into slices and serve hot with plenty of napkins.

Rosemary and Lemon Zest Fougasse

Fougasse is a leaf-shaped bread with decorative cuts. This is one of the breads I make in limited quantities but it's very popular with my customers. It is beautiful, unique, and wonderful for sharing with friends or gracing the dinner table at a special gathering.

MAKES 1 FOUGASSE

PREP TIME: 15 minutes (5 minutes to mix the dough, 5 minutes to fold the dough, and 5 minutes to shape the dough)

INACTIVE TIME: 20 minutes to rest, 1 hour 30 minutes to rise, 30 to 40 minutes to proof the dough and preheat the oven

BAKE TIME: 20 to 25 minutes

TOOLS NEEDED: thermometer, kitchen scale, large bowl, kitchen towel, 16-by-24-inch rimmed baking sheet, pastry brush, pizza cutter

FOR THE DOUGH
8 grams instant yeast
375 grams water
500 grams all-purpose flour
10 grams salt
Oil, for greasing the pan

FOR THE FOUGASSE TOPPING
¼ cup olive oil, divided
Zest of 1 lemon (I like Meyer lemons best)
2 rosemary sprigs, chopped
2 tablespoons flaky sea salt

CONTINUED →

1. CREATE THE DOUGH: Follow the Master Recipe for No-Knead Bread (page 28) through step 8.

2. SHAPE: Oil a 16-by-24-inch rimmed baking sheet. Pull your dough out of the bowl and drop it directly onto the sheet. Pour half of the olive oil over the dough and start gently stretching the dough toward the bottom two corners of the pan and pull the top edge toward the top of the pan to form a large triangle shape.

3. MIX: Combine the lemon zest, chopped rosemary, and the remaining olive oil in a small bowl. Use a pastry brush to spread the lemon-rosemary oil evenly all over the surface of the fougasse dough. Sprinkle the sea salt all over the top.

4. PROOF: Let the dough proof for 30 to 40 minutes.

5. PREHEAT: While the dough is proofing, preheat the oven to 450°F and set the oven rack in the center position.

6. DECORATE: Fougasse is cut into a beautiful leaf shape. Using a pizza cutter, make a large cut up the center of the dough, making sure not to cut all of the way through. Pull the dough apart a bit to make the cut a little wider. Now make 3 cuts on each side of the center cut, arcing upward like the veins of a leaf, and pull the dough apart like you did with the first cut.

7. BAKE: Bake for 20 to 25 minutes, until the fougasse is golden and crisp. The aroma in your kitchen will be heaven.

8. ENJOY: Fougasse is best eaten as hot as you can stand it.

Chapter Four

Kneaded Breads

Multigrains, Whole Grains, and Flavored Loaves

In this chapter we will progress to kneaded breads. Kneading your dough gives you an opportunity to develop more structure in your bread and practice another skill: shaping. After the minimalism of creating the rustic, no-knead varieties, you may be longing to make loaves that have a more defined shape and structure. Kneading and shaping also allow you to have a loaf that you can "score," or slash with a razor blade, to decorate the top of your bread. Practicing these techniques will be the foundation for advancing your skills and producing more artistic, creative, and beautiful loaves. The recipes in this chapter incorporate a slightly longer rise, which gives them more flavor. Each recipe makes 2 loaves since as your bread gets better and you become more confident, you'll want to make even more of it! If you are still unsure how to tell if your loaf is fermented well or proofed perfectly, simply practice the previous chapter's recipes again before moving on.

Boule

Boule refers to the shape of this classic rustic bread, which is round. This recipe will get you started in the direction of creating more beautiful and creative breads now that you have the basics well in hand. We will advance you to kneading and development, shaping beautiful loaves, and scoring your breads. Once you feel comfortable, and after a bit of practice, enjoy playing with the other recipes in this chapter to introduce new flavors to your breads!

MAKES 2 LOAVES

PREP TIME: 25 minutes (5 minutes to mix the dough, 10 minutes to knead the dough, and 10 minutes to divide and shape the dough)

INACTIVE TIME: 1 hour to rest, 3 hours to rise, 1 to 2 hours to proof the dough and preheat the oven

BAKE TIME: 40 to 45 minutes

TOOLS NEEDED: thermometer, kitchen scale, large bowl, metal dough scraper, 2 round baskets, 2 kitchen towels, Dutch oven

8 grams instant yeast
720 grams water
1,000 grams all-purpose flour
20 grams salt

1. PREPARE: Find the ambient temperature of your kitchen with a thermometer. A great way to do this is to take the temperature of your flour while it is sitting out at room temperature. Take a look at the chart on page 21 to see what temperature water you need for your dough. I find the easiest way to get my water to the correct temperature is to fill a pitcher or jar with hot water and one with cold water from the tap. I pour the cold water into the hot water until I've reached the ideal temperature. The desired dough temperature here is 75°F.

2. SCALE: Weigh all of the ingredients separately before you begin. This helps keep everything accurate. Use smaller bowls for ingredients in smaller amounts, like yeast and salt, to get the most precise reading.

CONTINUED →

3. COMBINE: Disperse the yeast into the water with a gentle swish of your fingers, like making a bubble bath. Let it sit for a couple of minutes. You should see a light foaming from the yeast, letting you know that it is feeling lively and ready to go to work for you. Next, add the flour on top of the water and yeast. Last, sprinkle the salt on top of the flour. This keeps it from coming into direct contact with the yeast, which can inhibit the rise.

4. MIX: Mix by hand, or use a plastic dough scraper to help. When evenly combined, the mixture should come together relatively easily and produce a wet but firm dough.

5. REST: Let your dough relax for about 30 minutes so the flour can absorb the water a bit. This will make it easier to knead.

6. KNEAD: Flour your work space and scrape the dough out onto it. The way I describe kneading to my kids is to "push and fold!" Push forward into your dough with the heels of your hands, and then fold the elongated dough back toward you. Give the dough a quarter turn. Then push the dough away and fold it back again. Keep kneading until you can feel that the dough has tightened up and has gotten smoother, usually 5 to 10 minutes. Pop your dough back into the bowl.

7. RISE: Place a floured kitchen towel (or plastic wrap if that's what you have) over your bowl, and go enjoy your life for 3 hours.

8. CHECK: Now that your dough has risen for 3 hours, it should be noticeably lighter, larger, and filled with air bubbles. To double-check, fill a cup with water, pinch off a little ball of your dough, and drop it into the glass. It should float to the top, indicating that your dough is aerated. If it doesn't seem particularly buoyant, it might be a cold day at your house. Let it rise a bit longer and check it again in 30 minutes or so.

9. DIVIDE AND PRESHAPE: Using a metal dough scraper, pull your dough onto a floured countertop or bread board and divide it into 2 equal pieces. Take your dough scraper and round each piece of dough by sliding the scraper underneath the far side of the dough and pulling it toward you, making the underside of the dough pull tighter. Giving it a quarter turn each time, repeat this motion to round your dough until you have developed tension across the surface of your loaf, stopping before it becomes too tight and starts to tear.

10.BENCH REST: Rest your 2 rounded pieces of dough on the work surface for 30 minutes, which will give it time to relax before shaping. Dust with flour and lightly cover with a kitchen towel.

11.SHAPE: Sprinkle flour on your work surface. Too much flour and your dough will slide around and not have the tension needed to be shaped. Too little flour and your dough will stick to you and your work surface. Think of it as a thin veil of flour on your work surface. To start shaping, turn one of the dough rounds over so the smooth side is resting on the floured work surface. Grab the far side of the dough and fold it down a third to the center, sealing it into a seam. Continue like you did with the no-knead bread, folding it like a letter, turning a quarter turn, and folding like a letter again. Now turn the loaf over with the seam down and cup your hands around the base of the far side of the loaf, pulling it toward you and building the tension of the loaf. Give it a turn and recreate this pulling motion from all angles, building a balanced tension all over the loaf without tearing the skin of the dough. Repeat with the other round of dough.

12. PROOF: Place each dough round into a proofing basket lined with a floured kitchen towel, seam-side up, and let rise for 1 hour to 1 hour 30 minutes, until the dough feels airy, like a marshmallow. When pressed with a finger, it should leave an indent instead of springing back up.

13. PREHEAT: While the dough is proofing, place an empty Dutch oven inside the oven and preheat to 475°F. This may seem like a long time to preheat an oven, but great bread needs a thoroughly hot oven for success. This is the final rise before it hops into the oven.

14. CHECK: To test that the dough is well proofed, press a finger gently into the dough. If it feels airy and light (like a marshmallow), it's ready to bake. Needing more time for proofing is a common theme in baking bread. Don't let it worry you if your dough needs more time to rise! Feeling the dough and adapting to the timing needs every time you bake bread is the way to become a better baker, so let your senses guide you.

15. BAKE: Flour your work surface well and tip 1 dough round out of a basket onto it, seam-side down. Carefully pull your very hot Dutch oven out of the oven and place it on top of the stove with the lid next to it. Make 2 deep slashes in the top of the dough with a razor blade or lame, making a big X. This will allow your loaf to spring upward in all directions and rise while it bakes. Pick the dough up with your hands and gently drop it into the pot, seam-side down and be careful to avoid burning your hands. Cover the Dutch oven with the lid, slide it into the oven, and bake for 25 minutes.

16. CHECK: At 25 minutes, take the cover off the Dutch oven. You should see a pale blond loaf that has risen to meet you. Continue baking with the cover removed for another 15 to 20 minutes. Your loaf will get some color and develop a nice crust. The finished loaf should be golden brown and will sound hollow when you thump it with your fingers. If the loaf seems to be browning too quickly, turn your oven down to 450°F. Repeat to bake the second loaf.

17. COOL: Let cool on a wire rack for at least 30 minutes to let the interior crumb set and make it easier to slice. You've now made your first kneaded bread!

Common Problems & FAQs

Q: Why did my loaf deflate when I scored it and, after baking, come out flat?

A: This is caused by overproofing. Check that your water and dough temperatures are correct and not too hot. Make sure that you don't let your final proof go too long, especially if it's a hot day.

Q: Why didn't my dough hold up when I shaped it into a loaf?

A: This is an underdevelopment issue. Be sure to knead adequately so the dough will keep its structure in the oven. Knead the dough until it is nice and tight and can't stretch anymore.

Q: Why is my loaf a strange shape?

A: An odd final shape indicates uneven tension during shaping, which pulls the loaf in one direction. It could also mean that the final proof was not adequate. When a loaf is fully proofed, it will spring apart while it bakes in a relaxed way where you've scored it. An underproofed loaf will rip and explode in the oven where you've scored it, resulting in odd angles in the final loaf. Give the dough plenty of time to proof, and check to be sure the dough is light and airy before it goes into the oven.

Q: Why does my loaf have a large hole or holes in the crumb?

A: This is a shaping issue. Sometimes an air bubble gets trapped during shaping and expands in the oven. Try to shape tightly so you don't end up with an air bubble in your loaf.

Kneaded Batard

A batard is an oblong, football-shaped, or oval loaf, and with this recipe you will get some practice shaping one. This is a classic shape that many bread bakers find very beautiful.

MAKES 2 LOAVES

PREP TIME: 25 minutes (5 minutes to mix the dough, 10 minutes to knead the dough, and 10 minutes to divide and shape the dough)

INACTIVE TIME: 1 hour to rest, 3 hours to rise, 1 hour to 1 hour 30 minutes to proof the dough and preheat the oven

BAKE TIME: 40 to 45 minutes

TOOLS NEEDED: thermometer, kitchen scale, large bowl, metal dough scraper, 2 oval baskets, 2 kitchen towels, Dutch oven or baking stone or roasting pan

8 grams instant yeast
720 grams water
1,000 grams all-purpose flour
20 grams salt

1. CREATE THE DOUGH: Follow the Master Recipe for Kneaded Bread (page 56) through step 10.

2. SHAPE: To shape a batard, sprinkle a thin veil of flour on your work surface and place 1 piece of dough on the flour with the smooth side down. Fold the far side of your dough down to meet the center and seal it to itself. You should have two corners now at the top of the dough; fold each of these down to that seam, sealing them to the center of the dough. Rub your hands on your work surface to coat them with flour so your dough won't stick. Tuck the bottom corners in to the center like you did with the top corners, sealing them to the center of the dough. Pull the newly formed top of the dough down to meet the bottom, sealing the dough against itself and pressing along the edge of the seam with the heel of your hand. Be sure to make a tight seam on the bottom of the loaf by pressing it closed with the heel of your hand. You can now gently roll this cylindrical loaf, pressing slightly outward to create the tapered ends of the batard. Repeat with the second piece of dough.

CONTINUED →

3. PROOF: Place each dough round into a basket lined with a floured kitchen towel, seam-side up, and let rise for 1 hour to 1 hour 30 minutes.

4. PREHEAT: While the dough is proofing, place an empty Dutch oven inside the oven and preheat to 475°F.

5. BAKE: Flour your work surface well and tip 1 loaf out of a basket onto it, seam-side down. Carefully pull your very hot Dutch oven out of the oven and place it on top of the stove with the lid next to it. Make a deep slash from the top of the dough to the bottom with a razor blade or lame. Pick the dough up with your hands and gently drop it into the Dutch oven, seam-side down, and be careful to avoid burning your hands.

Cover the Dutch oven with the lid, slide it into the oven, and bake for 25 minutes.

6. CHECK: At 25 minutes, take the cover off the Dutch oven. You should see a pale blond loaf that has risen to meet you. Continue baking with the cover removed for another 15 to 20 minutes. Your loaf will get some color and develop a nice crust. The finished loaf should be golden brown and will sound hollow when you thump it with your fingers. If the loaf seems to be browning too quickly, turn your oven down to 450°F. Repeat to bake the second loaf.

7. COOL: Let cool on a wire rack for at least 30 minutes to let the interior crumb set and make it easier to slice.

Country Loaves

These country loaves introduce you to the addition of whole-wheat. Starting with a small amount of this flour is a great way to feel out the differences it makes in your dough. Whole-grain flour will absorb slightly more water than white flour, and this formula reflects that. Different flours vary, so try to feel your dough as you add the water, and adjust as needed. When you are ready for something a little different, try out the variation below that includes rye for its sweet, earthy notes.

MAKES 2 LOAVES

PREP TIME: 25 minutes (5 minutes to mix the dough, 10 minutes to knead the dough, and 10 minutes to divide and shape the dough)

INACTIVE TIME: 1 hour to rest, 3 hours to rise, 1 hour to 1 hour 30 minutes to proof and preheat the oven

BAKE TIME: 40 to 45 minutes

TOOLS NEEDED: thermometer, kitchen scale, large bowl, metal dough scraper, 2 oval or round baskets, 2 kitchen towels, Dutch oven

Country Wheat Variation

Follow the Master Recipe for Kneaded Bread (page 56) to create this bread, using the ingredient amounts listed and shaping it into a boule or batard as desired.

8 grams instant yeast
730 grams water
900 grams all-purpose flour
100 grams whole-wheat flour
20 grams salt

Country Multigrain Variation

Rye can also be challenging to work with due to its lack of gluten, which is why I've kept it to such a small amount in this multigrain dough. This way, the rye can impart its nuanced flavor without undermining the strength of the loaf. Use the ingredient amounts listed below.

8 grams instant yeast
730 grams water
850 grams all-purpose flour
100 grams whole-wheat flour
50 grams rye flour
20 grams salt

Country Raisin and Walnut Loaf

Once you are comfortable with a bit of whole grain in your loaf, we can move forward to including other elements, which opens up so many flavor possibilities. This is a favorite of mine, with the buttery texture of walnuts and nice sweetness from the raisins. It's delicious toasted and spread with butter. You can substitute pecans for the walnuts if you are feeling particularly fancy. Any dried fruit (I like dried cherries) works in these proportions, so feel free to be creative once you get the hang of it.

MAKES 2 LOAVES

PREP TIME: 25 minutes (5 minutes to mix the dough, 10 minutes to knead the dough, and 10 minutes to divide and shape the dough)

INACTIVE TIME: 1 hour to rest, 3 hours to rise, 1 hour to 1 hour 30 minutes to proof the dough and preheat the oven

BAKE TIME: 40 to 45 minutes

TOOLS NEEDED: thermometer, kitchen scale, large bowl, metal dough scraper, 2 oval or round baskets, 2 kitchen towels, Dutch oven

FOR THE DOUGH
8 grams instant yeast
730 grams water
900 grams all-purpose flour
100 grams whole-wheat flour
20 grams salt

FOR THE ADDITIONS
100 grams raisins
200 grams toasted walnuts, chopped

CONTINUED →

1. CREATE THE DOUGH: Follow the Master Recipe for Kneaded Bread (page 56) through step 6, using the ingredient amounts listed.

2. ADD: Get your hands wet first and then fold the raisins and walnuts into the dough. Continue folding until the nuts and fruit are evenly dispersed throughout the dough.

3. RISE: Place a floured kitchen towel (or plastic wrap if that's what you have) over your bowl, and let sit for 3 hours.

4. CHECK: After 3 hours, your dough should be noticeably lighter, larger, and filled with air bubbles. To double-check, fill a cup with water, pinch off a little ball of your dough, and drop it into the glass. It should float to the top, indicating that your dough is aerated. If it doesn't seem particularly buoyant, it might be a cold day at your house. Let it rise a bit longer and check it again in 30 minutes or so.

5. DIVIDE AND PRESHAPE: Using a metal dough scraper, pull your dough onto a floured countertop or bread board and divide it into 2 equal pieces. Take your dough scraper and round each piece of dough by sliding the scraper underneath the far side of the dough and pulling it toward you, making the underside of the dough pull tighter Giving it a quarter turn each time, repeat this motion to round your dough until you have developed tension across the surface of your loaf, stopping before it becomes too tight and starts to tear.

6. BENCH REST: Rest your 2 rounded pieces of dough on the work surface for 30 minutes, which will give it time to relax before shaping. Dust with flour and lightly cover with a kitchen towel.

7. SHAPE: Sprinkle flour on your work surface. Too much flour and your dough will slide around and not have the tension needed to be shaped. Too little flour and your dough will stick to you and your work surface, which will make you and your dough very upset. Think of it as a thin veil of flour on your work surface. To start shaping, turn one of the dough rounds over so the smooth side is resting on the floured work surface. Grab the far side of the dough and fold it down a third to the center, sealing it into a seam. Continue like you did with the no-knead bread, folding it like a letter, turning a quarter turn, and folding like a letter again. Now turn the loaf over with the seam down and cup your hands around the base of the far side of the loaf, pulling it toward you and building the tension of the loaf. Give it a turn and recreate this pulling motion from all angles, building a balanced tension all over the loaf without tearing the skin of the dough. Repeat with the other round of dough.

8. PROOF: Place each dough round into a proofing basket lined with a floured kitchen towel, seam-side up, and let rise for 1 hour to 1 hour 30 minutes, until the dough feels airy, like a marshmallow. When pressed with a finger, it should leave an indent instead of springing back up.

9. PREHEAT: While the dough is proofing, place an empty Dutch oven inside the oven and preheat to 475°F. This may seem like a long time to preheat an oven, but great bread needs a thoroughly hot oven for success. This is the final rise before it hops into the oven.

10.CHECK: To test that the dough is well proofed, press a finger gently into the dough. If it feels airy and light (like a marshmallow), it's ready to bake. Needing more time for proofing is a common theme in baking bread. Don't let it worry you if your dough needs more time to rise! Feeling the dough and adapting to the timing needs every time you bake bread is the way to become a better baker, so let your senses guide you.

11.BAKE: Flour your work surface well and tip 1 loaf out of a basket onto it, seam-side down. Carefully pull your very hot Dutch oven out of the oven and place it on top of the stove with the lid next to it. Make 2 deep slashes in the top of the dough with a razor blade or lame, making a big X. This will allow your loaf to spring upward in all directions and rise while it bakes. Pick the dough up with your hands and gently drop it into the Dutch oven seam-side down, and be careful to avoid burning your hands. Cover the Dutch oven with the lid, slide it into the oven, and bake for 25 minutes.

12.CHECK: At 25 minutes, take the cover off the Dutch oven. You should see a pale blond loaf that has risen to meet you. Continue baking with the cover removed for another 15 to 20 minutes. Your loaf will get some color and develop a nice crust. The finished loaf should be golden brown and will sound hollow when you thump it with your fingers. If the loaf seems to be browning too quickly, turn your oven down to 450°F. Repeat to bake the second loaf.

13.COOL: Let cool on a wire rack for at least 30 minutes to let the interior crumb set and make it easier to slice.

Country Parmesan and Black Pepper Loaf

I developed this loaf after a regular customer who is a cheesemaker began bringing me cheese when he picked up his bread each week. The cheeses he brings always vary, and I've discovered that different types—from golden Parmesan to alpine Swiss—make a wonderful addition. I prefer grated cheese over cubed cheese because I feel that large pieces of cheese compromise the overall crumb of the loaf.

MAKES 2 LOAVES

PREP TIME: 25 minutes (5 minutes to mix the dough, 10 minutes to knead the dough, and 10 minutes to divide and shape the dough)

INACTIVE TIME: 1 hour to rest, 3 hours to rise, 1 hour to 1 hour 30 minutes to proof the dough and preheat the oven

BAKE TIME: 40 to 45 minutes

TOOLS NEEDED: thermometer, kitchen scale, large bowl, metal dough scraper, 2 oval or round baskets, 2 kitchen towels, Dutch oven

FOR THE DOUGH
8 grams instant yeast
730 grams water
900 grams all-purpose flour
100 grams whole-wheat flour
20 grams salt

FOR THE ADDITIONS
250 grams grated Parmesan cheese
10 grams freshly cracked black pepper

CONTINUED ➔

1. CREATE THE DOUGH: Follow the Master Recipe for Kneaded Bread (page 56) through step 6, using the ingredient amounts listed.

2. ADD: Get your hands wet first and then fold the cheese and the pepper into the dough. Continue folding until the cheese is evenly dispersed throughout the dough.

3. RISE: Place a floured kitchen towel (or plastic wrap if that's what you have) over your bowl, and let sit for 3 hours.

4. CHECK: After 3 hours, your dough should be noticeably lighter, larger, and filled with air bubbles. To double-check, fill a cup with water, pinch off a little ball of your dough, and drop it into the glass. It should float to the top, indicating that your dough is aerated. If it doesn't seem particularly buoyant, it might be a cold day at your house. Let it rise a bit longer and check it again in 30 minutes or so.

5. DIVIDE AND PRESHAPE: Using a metal dough scraper, pull your dough onto a floured countertop or bread board and divide it into 2 equal pieces. Take your dough scraper and round each piece of dough by sliding the scraper underneath the far side of the dough and pulling it toward you, making the underside of the dough pull tighter. Giving it a quarter turn each time, repeat this motion to round your dough until you have developed tension across the surface of your loaf, stopping before it becomes too tight and starts to tear.

6. BENCH REST: Rest your 2 rounded pieces of dough on the work surface for 30 minutes, which will give it time to relax before shaping. Dust with flour and lightly cover with a kitchen towel.

7. SHAPE: Sprinkle flour on your work surface. Too much flour and your dough will slide around and not have the tension needed to be shaped. Too little flour and your dough will stick to you and your work surface, which will make you and your dough very upset. Think of it as a thin veil of flour on your work surface. To start shaping, turn one of the dough rounds over so the smooth side is resting on the floured work surface. Grab the far side of the dough and fold it down a third to the center, sealing it into a seam. Continue like you did with the no-knead bread, folding it like a letter, turning a quarter turn, and folding like a letter again. Now turn the loaf over with the seam down and cup your hands around the base of the far side of the loaf, pulling it toward you and building the tension of the loaf. Give it a turn and recreate this pulling motion from all angles, building a balanced tension all over the loaf without tearing the skin of the dough. Repeat with the other round of dough.

8. PROOF: Place each dough round into a proofing basket lined with a floured kitchen towel, seam-side up, and let rise for 1 hour to 1 hour 30 minutes, until the dough feels airy, like a marshmallow. When pressed with a finger, it should leave an indent instead of springing back up.

9. PREHEAT: While the dough is proofing, place an empty Dutch oven inside the oven and preheat to 475°F. This may seem like a long time to preheat an oven, but great bread needs a thoroughly hot oven for success. This is the final rise before it hops into the oven.

10. CHECK: To test that the dough is well proofed, press a finger gently into the dough. If it feels airy and light (like a marshmallow), it's ready to bake. Needing more time for proofing is a common theme in baking bread. Don't let it worry you if your dough needs more time to rise! Feeling the dough and adapting to the timing needs every time you bake bread is the way to become a better baker, so let your senses guide you.

11. BAKE: Flour your work surface well and tip 1 loaf out of a basket onto it, seam-side down. Carefully pull your very hot Dutch oven out of the oven and place it on top of the stove with the lid next to it. Make 2 deep slashes in the top of the dough with a razor blade or lame, making a big X. This will allow your loaf to spring upward in all directions and rise while it bakes. Pick the dough up with your hands and gently drop it into the pot, seam-side down and be careful to avoid burning your hands. Cover the Dutch oven with the lid, slide it into the oven, and bake for 25 minutes.

12. CHECK: At 25 minutes, take the cover off the Dutch oven. You should see a pale blond loaf that has risen to meet you. Continue baking with the cover removed for another 15 to 20 minutes. Your loaf will get some color and develop a nice crust. The finished loaf should be golden brown and will sound hollow when you thump it with your fingers. If the loaf seems to be browning too quickly, turn your oven down to 450°F. Repeat to bake the second loaf.

13. COOL: Let cool on a wire rack for at least 30 minutes to let the interior crumb set and make it easier to slice.

Kindergarten Honey Wheat Bread

This is the bread I make with preschool- and kindergarten-age children in our homeschool. In Waldorf schools, it's common to bake bread weekly with the class, and I adapted this recipe from a Waldorf classroom bread book. The honey makes for a tender and sweet dough, which is very versatile—bake it into a loaf or to let the children shape it into rolls or other creative shapes. Kneading dough is a great way to direct a child with lots of extra energy, and teaching kids the magic of baking bread is both practical and fun. I usually do the initial mix and begin the kneading process until the dough is no longer sticky before passing the dough on to a child. While kids seem to like being messy, you would be surprised how distressed they can get when they have sticky dough hands. The quantity of yeast is higher here than in the other kneaded loaves in this chapter, so it doesn't take so long to make. This accommodates the shorter attention span of children and the typical lesson period. Once they learn how to bake bread, your children will be very impressed with themselves.

**MAKES 2 LOAVES OR
14 TO 16 SMALL ROLLS**

PREP TIME: 25 minutes (5 minutes to mix the dough, 10 minutes to knead the dough, and 10 minutes to divide and shape the dough)

INACTIVE TIME: 30 minutes to rest, 1 hour 30 minutes to rise, 1 hour to proof the dough and preheat the oven

BAKE TIME: 40 to 45 minutes

TOOLS NEEDED: thermometer, kitchen scale, large bowl, kitchen towel, 12-by-18-inch rimmed baking sheet, parchment paper

FOR THE DOUGH
16 grams instant yeast
600 grams water
500 grams all-purpose flour
500 grams whole-wheat flour
20 grams salt
120 grams honey
50 grams oil

FOR THE EGG WASH (OPTIONAL)
1 egg
2 tablespoons milk

1. CREATE THE DOUGH: Follow the Master Recipe for Kneaded Bread (page 56) through step 6, using the ingredient amounts listed and mixing with the honey and oil.

2. RISE: Place a floured kitchen towel (or plastic wrap if that's what you have) over your bowl, and go enjoy your life for 1 hour 30 minutes.

3. DIVIDE AND SHAPE: Divide the dough into 2 equal pieces, if making 2 loaves, or 14 to 16 pieces, if making small rolls. (If you are baking with children, you can let them shape the pieces into whatever shapes their hearts desire.) It's a very forgiving dough, and I have seen many creative shapes, from snakes and snails to rounds and hearts. Place the loaves or rolls on a 16-by-24-inch rimmed baking sheet lined with parchment paper.

4. PROOF: Let proof for 1 hour, until the dough feels airy, like a marshmallow. When pressed with a finger, it should leave an indent instead of springing back up.

5. PREHEAT: While the dough is proofing, preheat the oven to 375°F. Please note that the temperature is considerably lower than I call for in the master method because this is a softer bread.

6. BRUSH: After proofing, brush the loaves or rolls with water, or brush with the egg wash if shiny bread is desired.

7. BAKE: Bake for 40 to 45 minutes. The bread should be golden brown and will sound hollow when you thump it with your fingers.

8. COOL: Let cool on a wire rack for at least 30 minutes to let the interior crumb set. Serving this with butter and honey always goes over well.

Brown Sugar Spice Oatmeal Bread

This was one of the first recipes that I developed for myself, and which I now make for my bakery. This bread came about because I would make a big batch of cinnamon and brown sugar oatmeal at the beginning of each week. Eventually I would fold unused oatmeal into a loaf that we could make breakfast toast out of. A piece of buttery toast that tastes like a comforting bowl of oatmeal on a cold morning is a magical thing, and it is great, hearty fuel for splashing in puddles all day long. The moisture from the oatmeal makes for a wonderful texture in this bread.

MAKES 2 LOAVES

PREP TIME: 25 minutes (5 minutes to mix the dough, 10 minutes to knead the dough, and 10 minutes to divide and shape the dough)

INACTIVE TIME: 1 hour to rest, 3 hours to rise, 1 to 2 hours to proof the dough and preheat the oven

BAKE TIME: 45 minutes

TOOLS NEEDED: thermometer, kitchen scale, large bowl, medium bowl, kitchen towel, metal dough scraper, 2 (9-by-5-by-3-inch) loaf pans, parchment paper

FOR THE DOUGH
8 grams instant yeast
700 grams water
800 grams all-purpose flour
200 grams whole-wheat flour
20 grams salt
Butter, oil, or cooking spray, for greasing the pans

FOR THE ADDITIONS
150 grams rolled oats, cooked according to the package directions
100 grams brown sugar
5 grams cinnamon

FOR THE EGG WASH (OPTIONAL)
1 egg
2 tablespoons milk

CONTINUED →

1. CREATE THE DOUGH: Follow the Master Recipe for Kneaded Bread (page 56) through step 6, using the ingredient amounts listed.

2. MIX: Mix together the oatmeal, brown sugar, and cinnamon in a medium bowl. Get your hands wet first and then fold the oatmeal mixture into the dough. Continue folding until the mixture is evenly dispersed throughout the dough.

3. RISE: Place a floured kitchen towel (or plastic wrap if that's what you have) over your bowl, and go enjoy your life for 3 hours.

4. CHECK: Now that your dough has risen for 3 hours, it should be noticeably lighter, larger, and filled with air bubbles. To double-check, fill a cup with water, pinch off a little ball of your dough, and drop it into the glass. It should float to the top, indicating that your dough is aerated. If it doesn't seem particularly buoyant, it might be a cold day at your house. Let it rise a bit longer and check it again in 30 minutes or so.

5. DIVIDE AND PRESHAPE: Using a metal dough scraper, pull your dough onto a floured countertop or bread board and divide it into 2 equal pieces. Take your dough scraper and round each piece of dough by sliding the scraper underneath the far side of the dough and pulling it toward you, making the underside of the dough pull tighter. Giving it a quarter turn

each time, repeat this motion to round your dough until you have developed tension across the surface of your loaf, stopping before it becomes too tight and starts to tear.

6. BENCH REST: Rest your 2 rounded pieces of dough on the work surface for 30 minutes, which will give it time to relax before shaping. Dust with flour and lightly cover with a kitchen towel.

7. SHAPE: Sprinkle a thin veil of flour on your work surface, and place 1 piece of the dough on top of the flour with the smooth side down. Fold the far side of your dough down to meet the center, and seal it to itself. You should have two corners now at the top of the dough. Fold each of these down to that seam, sealing them to the center of the dough. Rub your hands on your work surface to coat them with flour so your dough won't stick. Tuck the bottom corners in to the center, like you did with the top corners, sealing them to the center of the dough. Pull the newly formed top of the dough down to meet the bottom, sealing the dough against itself and pressing along the edge of the seam with the heel of your hand. Be sure to make a tight seam on the bottom of the loaf by pressing it closed with the heel of your hand. You can now gently roll this cylindrical loaf, pressing slightly to create the tapered ends of the batard. Repeat with the second piece of dough.

8. PROOF: Gently place the dough into 2 greased loaf pans, seam-side down. Proof for 1 to 2 hours, until the dough starts to crest or "mushroom" up out of the top of the pan.

9. PREHEAT: While the dough is proofing, preheat the oven to 375°F. Place your oven rack on the bottom level of the oven.

10. BRUSH: After the dough is proofed, if using the egg wash, whisk the egg with the milk in a bowl and brush the mixture onto the top of the loaves before baking. If you are not using the egg wash, brush the top of the loaves generously with water to keep them from forming a hard top.

11. BAKE: Bake the loaves for 45 minutes. At 20 minutes, check the oven to make sure the top of each loaf isn't browning too quickly. If it is, you can protect it by tenting foil over the top of each loaf. The finished loaves should be golden brown and will sound hollow when you thump them with your fingers.

12. COOL: Remove your loaves from the pans right after taking them out of the oven and let cool on a wire rack for at least 30 minutes before slicing. If you leave the bread in the pan to cool, the crust will steam and get soggy, and the loaves will be difficult to remove from the pans.

Chapter Five

Enriched Breads

Brioche, Cinnamon Rolls, Babka, Challah, and Variations

Now that you are confident in your rising, proofing, and kneading skills, it's time to have some fun. This chapter provides even more bread-baking possibilities with enriched doughs. An "enriched" bread is one that incorporates ingredients that have a softening effect on the dough. These are usually "rich" ingredients, like butter, sugar, milk, and eggs. These soft and sweet doughs create many of our favorite breads for giving as gifts, celebrating holidays, and enjoying with our friends and family.

Brioche

Master Recipe: Enriched Bread:

This formula makes a simple brioche, a beautifully soft and lightly sweet loaf. I've developed this recipe so that it can be mixed by hand, even though most brioche recipes call for a mixer. This sweet bread makes excellent French toast and is a delicious treat on the weekend. Many of my customers like to pick up a brioche on Saturday for a lazy Sunday breakfast. Making your own is a sweet luxury.

MAKES 2 LOAVES

PREP TIME: 25 to 30 minutes (10 minutes to mix the dough, 5 to 10 minutes to knead the dough, and 10 minutes to divide and shape the dough)

INACTIVE TIME: 20 to 30 minutes to rest, 1 hour 30 minutes to 2 hours to rise, 1 hour 30 minutes to 2 hours to proof the dough and preheat the oven

BAKE TIME: 35 to 40 minutes

TOOLS NEEDED: kitchen scale, large bowl, kitchen towel, metal dough scraper, 2 (9-by-5-by-3-inch) loaf pans, pastry brush

FOR THE DOUGH

156 grams whole milk
256 grams whole eggs
72 grams sugar
6 grams yeast
180 grams very soft butter
600 grams all-purpose flour
12 grams salt
Butter, oil, or cooking spray, for greasing the pans

FOR THE EGG WASH

1 egg
2 tablespoons water

CONTINUED →

1. SCALE: Weigh all of the ingredients before you begin. In this case, the milk and eggs can be cold from the refrigerator, but the butter needs to be very soft (not melted) so that it can be incorporated into the dough by hand.

2. COMBINE: Combine the milk, eggs, sugar, yeast, and butter in a large bowl using a whisk or a fork.

3. MIX: Add the flour and salt on top of the wet ingredients and mix by hand, feeling that the ingredients are well combined, until a smooth, even, wet dough is produced. Don't worry if it seems very relaxed. The soft butter will firm up with the colder ingredients in the dough.

4. REST: Cover the dough with a floured kitchen towel, and let it rest for 20 to 30 minutes while the flour absorbs the liquid ingredients.

5. KNEAD: Flour your work surface and turn the dough out onto it. Knead the dough by pushing forward into the dough with the heels of your hands and then folding the elongated dough back toward you. Give it a quarter turn, push the dough away, and fold it back again. Keep with it until you can feel that the dough has tightened up and has gotten smoother, 5 to 10 minutes.

6. RISE: Place the dough in a large bowl and cover with a floured kitchen towel or plastic wrap and let rise for 1 hour 30 minutes to 2 hours.

7. DIVIDE AND SHAPE: Using a metal dough scraper, divide the dough into 2 pieces and shape each into a simple loaf shape: Fold the far side (12 o'clock) down to the middle, sealing the dough against itself. Fold the bottom up to meet the seam and seal it. This is a letter fold. Turn the dough so the seam is vertical, and do the letter fold again, sealing the dough to itself. You should have a nice little rounded square shape. Place your loaves into 2 greased loaf pans.

8. PROOF: Let the loaves proof for 1 hour 30 minutes to 2 hours, until the dough "mushrooms" above the edges of each pan and feels light and airy.

9. PREHEAT: While the dough is proofing, preheat the oven to 375°F.

10. BAKE: Make an egg wash by whisking the egg with the water. Brush it over the tops of the loaves with a pastry brush. Bake the loaves for 35 to 40 minutes. The finished loaves should be golden brown and will sound hollow when you thump them with your fingers.

11. COOL: Let cool in the pans for about 10 minutes, then transfer the loaves from the pans to a cooling rack for 20 more minutes before slicing.

MAKING BRIOCHE DOUGH

Mixing and kneading brioche dough by hand.

Common Problems and FAQs

Q: Why was my loaf dense on the bottom and light on the top?

A: The dough may have needed more time to proof fully. Make sure you give it adequate time and watch for the signs of a well-risen dough (light and puffy).

Q: Why did my loaf tear along the side/top of the loaf in the oven?

A: This is an underproofing issue. The loaf needs a longer proof in the pan until it is high above the edges of the pan. This way it won't tear apart from springing too much farther in the oven.

Q: Why did my loaf rise a lot and then collapse in the oven?

A: This is a result of overproofing. If the dough has risen for too long, it will lose its structure and collapse. Check on your loaf during proofing to make sure it doesn't overproof.

Q: Why was my finished product wet/raw inside?

A: This can happen with braided/twisted/rolled doughs. Two factors can cause this: One is rolling extremely tight, which makes it difficult for the bread to rise. Another is an insufficient final proof or an extremely wet filling. Be careful with your fillings. Follow the recipe instead of improvising, don't twist or roll extremely tightly, and be sure to give enough time for the final rise.

Orange Blossom Special Brioche

This brioche variation is one that I make for my customers from about Valentine's Day to Mother's Day, when it's beautiful citrus season here in California and the air is perfumed with opening blossoms. I consider these two holidays "French toast holidays," which nicely bookend the season for this loaf. If you want to make someone you love feel extra special, this brioche loaf will do the job. Orange blossom water adds a delicate floral note to this bread. It can be found easily online and in many Middle Eastern grocery stores.

MAKES 2 LOAVES

PREP TIME: 25 minutes (10 minutes to mix the dough, 5 minutes to knead the dough, and 10 minutes to divide and shape the dough)

INACTIVE TIME: 20 to 30 minutes to rest, 1 hour 30 minutes to 2 hours to rise, 1 hour 30 minutes to 2 hours to proof the dough and preheat the oven

BAKE TIME: 35 to 40 minutes

TOOLS NEEDED: kitchen scale, large bowl, kitchen towel, metal dough scraper, 2 (9-by-5-by-3-inch) loaf pans, pastry brush

FOR THE DOUGH

140 grams whole milk
256 grams whole eggs
80 grams wildflower honey
Zest of 2 oranges
10 grams orange blossom water (optional)
6 grams yeast
180 grams very soft butter
600 grams all-purpose flour
12 grams salt

FOR THE EGG WASH

1 egg
2 tablespoons water

Follow the Master Recipe for Enriched Bread (page 82) to create this bread, using the ingredient amounts listed.

Brioche Cinnamon Rolls

Brioche dough makes gorgeous cinnamon rolls. These are so soft, fluffy, and tender, and the filling is perfect with a little extra cinnamon. One-third of the filling is put in the bottom of the pan so when the rolls are baked and you invert them onto a platter, the rolls will have a lovely, sweet, caramelized glaze on top. I love to make these for Christmas morning, a tradition in our family, as well as for birthdays or any time a special breakfast is necessary.

MAKES 12 ROLLS

PREP TIME: 25 minutes (10 minutes to mix the dough, 5 minutes to knead the dough, and 10 minutes to divide and shape the dough)

INACTIVE TIME: 20 to 30 minutes to rest, 1 hour 30 minutes to 2 hours to rise, 2 hours or overnight to chill (optional), 1 hour 30 minutes to 2 hours to proof the dough and preheat the oven

BAKE TIME: 35 to 40 minutes

TOOLS NEEDED: kitchen scale, large bowl, medium bowl, kitchen towel, metal dough scraper, rolling pin, rubber spatula, 9-by-13-inch nonstick roasting pan

FOR THE DOUGH
156 grams whole milk
256 grams whole eggs
72 grams sugar
6 grams yeast
180 grams very soft butter
600 grams all-purpose flour
12 grams salt

FOR THE FILLING
110 grams soft butter
250 grams brown sugar
15 grams cinnamon
1 tablespoon vanilla extract
Flaky sea salt for topping (optional)

1. CREATE THE DOUGH: Follow the Master Recipe for Enriched Bread (page 82) through step 6, using the ingredient amounts listed. After the rise, the dough can be chilled in the refrigerator for 2 hours to overnight, to make it easier to roll out.

2. MAKE THE FILLING: In a medium bowl, combine the butter, sugar, cinnamon, and vanilla with a spatula and set aside.

3. ROLL OUT: Flour your work surface. Take the dough from the refrigerator, if chilled, and roll it out with a rolling pin to a rectangle about 24 inches by 8 inches. The longer side should be horizontal.

4. SHAPE: Using a rubber spatula, spread about ¾ of the filling over the dough, covering the surface but leaving a small strip of dough uncovered on the long side farthest from you; you will use this to seal the edge of the dough. Gently roll up the dough, pushing the edge of the dough away from you and rolling it up like a yoga mat. Seal the seam by pressing the dough together. Using a metal dough scraper, cut the spiral into 12 (2-inch) rolls. If your roasting pan doesn't have a nonstick surface, line it with parchment paper or aluminum foil. Spread the remaining cinnamon-sugar filling over the bottom of the pan, then place the rolls into the pan cut-side up, spacing them evenly apart so that they have room to rise.

5. PROOF: At this point, you have two options: You can proof and bake the rolls, or you can refrigerate them from 2 hours to overnight and then proof and bake them. Whichever option you choose, proof for 1 hour 30 minutes to 2 hours, until they are puffy and full of air and feel like a marshmallow. When pressed with a finger, it should leave an indent instead of springing back up.

6. PREHEAT: While the dough is proofing, preheat your oven to 375°F.

7. BAKE: Bake for 35 to 40 minutes, until browned on top. Take a sheet pan or large platter, place it over the roasting pan, and invert to release the cinnamon rolls.

8. COOL: Let cool for 30 minutes before serving. I like to top them with flaky sea salt, but this is optional.

Shaping and cutting brioche cinnamon rolls.

Cinnamon Raisin Swirl Bread

This bread is something wonderful to have in the house. In the winter months, when motivation to get out of bed is very low and the daylight hours get short, knowing you have cinnamon raisin toast to wake up to can make it happen. This one also makes an excellent gift for someone going through a tough time. It's almost a miracle how much a small kindness such as this can mean. Make these loaves and share one with someone who needs a warm hug.

MAKES 2 LOAVES

PREP TIME: 25 minutes (10 minutes to mix the dough, 5 minutes to knead the dough, and 10 minutes to divide and shape the dough)

INACTIVE TIME: 20 to 30 minutes to rest, 1 hour 30 minutes to 2 hours to rise, 2 hours or overnight to chill (optional), 1 hour 30 minutes to 2 hours to proof the dough and preheat the oven

BAKE TIME: 35 to 40 minutes

TOOLS NEEDED: kitchen scale, large bowl, kitchen towel, metal dough scraper, 2 (9-by-5-by-3-inch) loaf pans, rolling pin, pastry brush

FOR THE DOUGH

156 grams whole milk
256 grams whole eggs
72 grams sugar
6 grams yeast
180 grams very soft butter
600 grams all-purpose flour
12 grams salt
80 grams raisins
Butter, oil, or cooking spray, for greasing the pans

FOR THE FILLING

100 grams sugar
8 grams cinnamon

FOR THE EGG WASH

1 egg
2 tablespoons water

CONTINUED →

1. CREATE THE DOUGH: Follow the Master Recipe for Enriched Bread (page 82) through step 6, using the ingredient amounts listed.

2. DIVIDE AND PRESHAPE: Grease 2 loaf pans or line them with parchment. Divide the dough into 2 equal pieces. Using a rolling pin, roll out each piece of dough into a rectangle approximately 8 by 16 inches, with the shorter side horizontal and closest to you. (Feel free to chill the dough if you feel that it's warm and difficult/sticky to roll out, but it's not as vital as with the cinnamon roll recipe since you won't be attempting to cut perfect spirals with a wet filling.)

3. BRUSH: Make the egg wash: Mix together the egg and water. Brush the dough rectangles lightly with the egg wash, reserving any leftover egg wash to brush the tops of the dough before baking. Combine the sugar and cinnamon, and sprinkle the mixture evenly over the dough. Roll up the rectangles from the shorter side, rolling away from you like a yoga mat. Place each loaf with the seam-side down into the prepared loaf pans.

4. PROOF: Proof for 1 hour 30 minutes to 2 hours, until the loaves "mushroom" well above the edges of the pans.

5. PREHEAT: While the dough is proofing, preheat the oven to 375°F.

6. BAKE: After proofing, brush the tops of the loaves with the remaining egg wash. Bake for 35 to 40 minutes. The finished loaves should be golden brown and will sound hollow when you thump them with your fingers.

7. COOL: Let cool in the pans for about 10 minutes, then transfer the loaves from the pans to a cooling rack for 20 more minutes before slicing.

Chocolate Babka

Babka is a sweet bread with chocolate filling. The dough is rolled up with the chocolate much like the cinnamon swirl loaf, but then the dough is halved and twisted and braided in such a way that the result is a striking, swirling, marbled masterpiece. It makes the ultimate hostess gift, as memorialized in the classic episode of *Seinfeld* with the phrase "Nothing beats a babka!"

MAKES 2 LOAVES

PREP TIME: 25 minutes (10 minutes to mix the dough, 5 minutes to knead the dough, and 10 minutes to divide and shape the dough)

INACTIVE TIME: 20 to 30 minutes to rest, 1 hour 30 minutes to 2 hours to rise, 2 hours to chill, 1 hour 30 minutes to 2 hours to proof the dough and preheat the oven

BAKE TIME: 35 to 40 minutes

TOOLS NEEDED: kitchen scale, large bowl, kitchen towel, metal dough scraper, saucepan, 12-by-18-inch baking sheet, 2 (9-by-5-by-3-inch) loaf pans, rubber spatula, pastry brush

FOR THE DOUGH

145 grams whole milk
205 grams whole eggs
60 grams sugar
5 grams yeast
150 grams very soft butter
500 grams all-purpose flour
10 grams salt
Butter, oil, or cooking spray, for greasing the pans

FOR THE FILLING

85 grams cocoa powder
198 grams sugar
227 grams cream
113 grams salted butter
1 tablespoon vanilla

CONTINUED →

1. CREATE THE DOUGH: Follow the Master Recipe for Enriched Bread (page 82) through step 6, using the ingredient amounts listed.

2. CHILL: After the first rise, cover the bowl with plastic wrap and refrigerate the dough for 2 hours. Chilling the dough allows it to be rolled out, shaped, and cut without sticking and making a big mess.

3. MAKE THE FILLING: While the dough is chilling, make the chocolate filling. I use my recipe for hot fudge, which may not be very authentic, but it has the most fantastic texture and works well with the dough. In a saucepan over medium heat, whisk together the cocoa powder, sugar, and cream until well combined and simmering. Add the butter and vanilla and stir until the butter melts. Turn off the heat and continue whisking until the mixture becomes shiny. Chill for at least 30 minutes in the refrigerator, until the filling is thick and spreadable.

4. DIVIDE AND PRESHAPE: Divide the dough into 2 equal pieces. Using a rolling pin, roll out each piece of dough into a rectangle as thin as you can get it, approximately 9 by 16 inches, with the shorter side horizontal and closest to you. The thinner the dough, the more contrast you will get with lots of swirls of chocolate. Using a rubber spatula, spread 1 dough rectangle with half of the fudge filling, covering the surface but leaving a small strip of dough uncovered on the long side farthest from you; you will use this to seal the edge of the dough. Gently roll up the dough, pushing the edge of the dough away from you and rolling it up like a yoga mat. Seal the seam by pressing the dough together. Repeat with the other piece of dough, using the rest of the fudge filling, and transfer both babka ropes to a baking sheet. Put them in the freezer for 15 minutes to firm them up, which will make them easier to cut.

5. SHAPE: Grease 2 loaf pans or line them with parchment. Take out the chilled ropes and use a sharp knife to cut each in half lengthwise. Take 2 halves and twist them around each other as much as possible (this creates the swirling marbling effect inside the dough) and place the twist into one of the loaf pans, folding and twisting to fit. Repeat with the other 2 halves and place into the other loaf pan.

6. PROOF: Let proof for 1 hour 30 minutes to 2 hours, until the dough is just reaching the top of the pan. (The dough won't rise as high as the Cinnamon Raisin Swirl Bread, page 92.)

7. PREHEAT: While the dough is proofing, preheat the oven to 375°F.

8. BAKE: Bake for 35 to 40 minutes. The finished loaves should be golden brown and will sound hollow when you thump them with your fingers.

9. COOL: Let cool in the pans for about 10 minutes, then transfer the loaves from the pans to a cooling rack for 20 more minutes before slicing.

HOW TO TWIST CHOCOLATE BABKA

Shaping and twisting the babka.

Challah

Challah is a traditional Jewish bread made for the Sabbath and other holidays. It's a beautiful and festive braided loaf with a shiny crust. My kids love when I make this bread because of its striking appearance. I love making it because the firm-yet-supple dough is so fun to work with.

MAKES 1 LARGE BRAIDED LOAF

PREP TIME: 25 minutes (10 minutes to mix the dough, 5 minutes to knead the dough, and 10 minutes to divide and shape the dough)

INACTIVE TIME: 40 to 50 minutes to rest, 1 hour 30 minutes to 2 hours to rise, 1 hour 30 minutes to 2 hours to proof the dough and preheat the oven

BAKE TIME: 35 to 45 minutes

TOOLS NEEDED: kitchen scale, large bowl, kitchen towel, metal dough scraper, 16-by-24-inch rimmed baking sheet, parchment paper, pastry brush

FOR THE DOUGH
145 grams whole milk
205 grams whole eggs
80 grams honey
5 grams yeast
30 grams vegetable oil
500 grams all-purpose flour
10 grams salt

FOR THE EGG WASH
1 egg
2 tablespoons water

CONTINUED →

1. CREATE THE DOUGH: Follow the Master Recipe for Enriched Bread (page 82) through step 6, using the ingredient amounts listed.

2. DIVIDE AND SHAPE: Line a baking sheet with parchment paper. Divide the dough into 3 equal parts and let rest for 20 minutes. Take each piece and roll it between your hands and the work surface into ropes about 12 inches long (just like making snakes out of Play-Doh back in the day). There are many ornate options for braiding challah, but let's start with a simple 3-strand braid. Arrange the strands next to each other vertically. Press the 3 strands together at the top. Pick up the strand on the right and cross it over the center strand; this strand is now in the center. Then, take the left strand and cross it over the center, arriving as the new center strand. Keep crossing each side over the center until the dough gets too short to do it. Press the strands together at the bottom, and transfer to the prepared baking sheet.

3. PROOF: Make the egg wash by mixing together the egg and water. Brush the dough lightly with the egg wash using a pastry brush, reserving any left over for brushing before you bake. Cover lightly with plastic wrap. Proof for 1 hour 30 minutes to 2 hours, until very puffed and light and airy.

4. PREHEAT: While the dough is proofing, preheat the oven to 350°F.

5. BAKE: Brush the dough with the remaining egg wash. Bake for 35 to 45 minutes. The finished loaf should be golden brown and will sound hollow when you thump it with your fingers.

6. COOL: Let cool on a wire rack for at least 30 minutes to let the interior crumb set and make it easier to slice.

HOW TO BRAID CHALLAH BREAD

Braid simply by placing the right and left strands alternately towards the center.

Springtime Challah Snails

This is another recipe I love to make with my kids. The dough is so soft and forgiving that it's very kid-friendly. These snails are a great project for a kids' class and can pair with a nature-focused lesson or story time while the dough rises. (My favorite story to pair with it is Eric Carle's *The Tiny Seed*, which has a profound message while teaching children about seeds and flowers.) Sprinkling seeds over the top of these rolls is a sweet touch that brings everything full circle.

MAKES 6 TO 8 SNAIL ROLLS

PREP TIME: 25 minutes (10 minutes to mix the dough, 5 minutes to knead the dough, and 10 minutes to divide and shape the dough)

INACTIVE TIME: 20 to 30 minutes to rest, 1 hour 30 minutes to 2 hours to rise, 1 hour to 1 hour 30 minutes to proof the dough and preheat the oven

BAKE TIME: 25 to 35 minutes

TOOLS NEEDED: kitchen scale, large bowl, kitchen towel, metal dough scraper, 16-by-24-inch rimmed baking sheet, parchment paper, scissors, pastry brush

FOR THE DOUGH
145 grams whole milk
205 grams whole eggs
80 grams honey
5 grams yeast
30 grams vegetable oil
500 grams all-purpose flour
10 grams salt

FOR THE EGG WASH
1 egg
2 tablespoons water

FOR THE TOPPING (OPTIONAL)
Flaxseed, sunflower seeds,
   or poppy seeds

CONTINUED →

Rolling up a sweet little snail.

1. CREATE THE DOUGH: Follow the Master Recipe for Enriched Bread (page 82) through step 6, using the ingredient amounts listed.

2. DIVIDE AND PRESHAPE: Line a baking sheet with parchment paper. Divide the dough into 6 or 8 equal pieces. Take each piece and roll it between your hands and the work surface into ropes about 8 inches long (just like making snakes out of Play-Doh back in the day). Coil each one into a snail shape, leaving the end free. Use scissors to and snip the little end into two little snail antennae. Place the snails on the prepared baking sheet.

3. PROOF: Make the egg wash by mixing together the egg and water. Brush each snail lightly with the egg wash, reserving any left over. Let the snails proof for 1 hour to 1 hour 30 minutes, until they are light and puffy. Brush them again with the reserved egg wash and sprinkle seeds over the top, if desired.

4. PREHEAT: While the dough is proofing, preheat the oven to 350°F.

5. BAKE: Bake for 25 to 35 minutes, until the snails are shiny and golden brown. Check often to see if they are done; smaller snails will cook more quickly than larger ones.

6. COOL: Let the snails cool on a wire rack for 30 minutes before serving.

Chapter Six

Breads with Pre-ferments and Sourdough Starter

If you have practiced through the previous chapters in this book, you should be feeling pretty confident in your beginner baking pursuits. You will use all of the different techniques you have learned in the previous chapters here: kneading, folding, and shaping. You will also use your intuitive skills of judging fermentation and final proof. If you feel happy with your abilities, it's time to move forward into incorporating pre-ferments in your doughs. This will help you achieve more depth of flavor and get comfortable with a longer dough-building process as well as assessing the pre-ferment. Once you can do this, you can build a sourdough starter and begin the journey toward making naturally leavened sourdough breads.

Bread with Pre-ferment (Poolish or Biga)

Whether you are working with poolish, biga, or even sourdough starter, there is a similar rhythm to the process. Working with a pre-ferment greatly improves the flavor and keeping quality of bread, and simply requires the forethought to prepare a starter the day before. This recipe is a starting point, creating a boule similar to the one you are familiar with from chapter 4, with the additional step of preparing a poolish the night before. It is simple to make, with wonderful results. Let's do it.

MAKES 2 LOAVES

PREP TIME: 25 minutes (10 minutes to mix the dough, 5 minutes to knead the dough, and 10 minutes to divide and shape the dough)

INACTIVE TIME: 12 to 16 hours to pre-ferment poolish, 1 hour to rest, 3 hours to rise, 1 hour to 1 hour 30 minutes to proof the dough and preheat the oven

BAKE TIME: 40 to 45 minutes

TOOLS NEEDED: large container with lid, thermometer, kitchen scale, large bowl, 2 kitchen towels, 2 round baskets, Dutch oven

FOR THE POOLISH
200 grams all-purpose flour
200 grams water
¼ teaspoon instant yeast

FOR THE DOUGH
3 grams instant yeast
400 grams poolish
720 grams water
1,000 grams all-purpose flour
20 grams salt

CONTINUED →

Weighing yeast and checking water temperature.

1. MAKE THE POOLISH: Combine the flour, water, and yeast in a large container with a lid at least 12 to 16 hours before you plan to start mixing your dough. The container should have adequate space for the poolish to double in size. Cover the container loosely with the lid. It's scary being awakened by your poolish expanding and shooting a plastic lid across the kitchen, trust me.

2. CHECK: After 12 hours, check to see if your poolish is full of air and has doubled in size.

3. PREPARE: Find the ambient temperature of your kitchen with a thermometer. A great way to do this is to take the temperature of your flour while it is sitting out at room temperature. Take a look at the chart on page 21 to see what temperature water you need for your dough. I find the easiest way to get my water to the correct temperature is to fill a pitcher or jar with hot water and one with cold water from the tap. I pour the cold water into the hot water until I've reached the ideal temperature. The desired dough temperature here is 76°F.

Mixing a dough with a pre-ferment.

4. SCALE: Weigh all of the ingredients separately before you begin. This helps keep everything accurate. Use smaller bowls for ingredients in smaller amounts, like yeast and salt, to get the most precise reading.

5. COMBINE: To make the dough, disperse the yeast and all of the poolish into the water with a gentle swish of your fingers, like making a bubble bath. Let it sit for a couple of minutes. You should see a light foaming from the yeast, letting you know that it is feeling lively and ready to go to work for you. Next, add the flour on top of the water and yeast. Last, sprinkle the salt on top of the flour. This keeps it

from coming into direct contact with the yeast, which can inhibit the rise.

6. MIX: I like to use my hands, or use a plastic dough scraper to help. The ingredients should come together easily and produce a wet but firm dough.

7. REST: Let your dough relax for about 30 minutes so the flour can absorb the water a bit, which will make it easier to knead.

8. KNEAD: Flour your work space and scrape the dough out onto it. Push forward into your dough with the heels of

CONTINUED →

your hands, and then fold the elongated dough back toward you. Give the dough a quarter turn, then push the dough away and fold it back again. Keep kneading until you can feel that the dough has tightened up and has gotten smoother, usually 5 to 10 minutes.

9. RISE AND FOLD: Let the dough rise for 3 hours. Halfway through the rise (after 1 hour 30 minutes), give the dough a few folds, using the folding technique you used in chapter 3. This will improve the strength and structure of the final dough.

10. CHECK: After 3 hours, the dough should be aerated and buoyant.

11. DIVIDE AND PRESHAPE: Divide the dough into 2 equal pieces. Gently turn your dough onto a floured countertop. The bottom, which was in contact with the bowl, will be facing up to you. If it is sticking to the bowl, use your hand or a plastic scraper to release it. Shape the dough by giving it a gentle letter fold: Fold the far side (12 o'clock) down to the middle, sealing the dough against itself. Now fold the bottom up to meet the seam and seal it. Turn the dough so this seam is vertical, and do that letter fold again, sealing the dough to itself. You should have a nice little rounded square shape. If the dough is nice and tight, you can stop there. If it seems very relaxed, you can give it another set of letter folds to create more tension, sealing the dough to itself.

12. BENCH REST: Rest the 2 pieces of dough on the work surface for 30 minutes. This will give them time to relax before shaping. Dust with flour and lightly cover with a kitchen towel.

13. SHAPE: Shape each piece into a boule. Flip the dough over and give it a letter fold, give it a quarter turn, and then give it another letter fold. Place the seam down and tighten up the loaf, pulling it across the work surface in a circular motion with your hands.

14. PROOF: Place each dough round into a basket lined with a floured kitchen towel, seam-side up. You are going to let this dough rise for 1 hour to 1 hour 30 minutes, until the dough feels airy, like a marshmallow. When pressed with a finger, it should leave an indent instead of springing back up. This is the final rise before it hops into the oven.

15. PREHEAT: While the dough is proofing, turn on your oven with an empty Dutch oven inside and let it preheat to 475°F.

16. CHECK: To test that the dough is well proofed, press a finger gently into the dough. If it seems springy and tight, it needs more time. If it feels airy and light, like a marshmallow, it's ready to bake. Needing more time for proofing is a common theme in baking bread. Don't let it worry you if your dough needs more time to rise! Feeling the dough and adapting to the timing needs every time you bake bread is the way to become a better baker, so let your senses guide you.

17.BAKE: Flour your work surface well and tip 1 loaf out of a basket onto it, seam-side down. Carefully pull your very hot Dutch oven out of the oven and place it on top of the stove with the lid next to it. Make 2 deep slashes in the top of the dough with a razor blade or lame, making a big X. This will allow your loaf to spring upward in all directions and rise while it bakes. Pick the dough up with your hands and gently drop it into the pot and be careful to avoid burning your hands. Cover the Dutch oven with the lid, slide it into the oven, and bake for 25 minutes.

18.CHECK: At 25 minutes, take the cover off the Dutch oven. You should see a pale blond loaf that has risen to meet you. Continue baking with the cover removed for another 15 to 20 minutes. Your loaf will get some color and develop a nice crust. The finished loaf should be golden brown and will sound hollow when you thump it with your fingers. If the loaf seems to be browning too quickly, turn your oven down to 450°F. Repeat to bake the second loaf.

19.COOL: Let cool on a wire rack for at least 30 minutes to let the interior crumb set and to make it easier to slice.

Common Problems and FAQs

Q: Why was my dough difficult to shape or very relaxed?

A: This could mean the gluten was not well developed and the dough should have been kneaded more. Knead the dough until it is smooth and feels stronger.

Q: Why did my loaf come out dense or heavy?

A: All other elements being correct, this will come back to the health of your starter or pre-ferment. Make sure that your starter is full of bubbles and well risen before using it in your dough. Using a starter or pre-ferment that is not airy and doubled in size will not create good bread.

Q: How can I get a better oven spring in my loaf?

A: This will go back to the health and vitality and strength of the starter. A strong starter has a consistent rise day after day and rises vigorously. If it is slow or sluggish and doesn't create many bubbles, it shouldn't be used to make bread yet.

Q: How can I get a more open crumb?

A: If your starter or pre-ferment is strong and you are still looking for a more open crumb, you may need to raise your water temperature 2° to 4° and push your fermentation and final proof a little bit further. If your other techniques and skills are good, this should help you achieve a more open crumb.

Baguettes with Poolish

Making a beautiful and perfect baguette can be a years-long quest, although it is deceptively simple in appearance. A straight, light, crisp-crusted, open-crumbed golden magic wand of bread can be elusive. Don't let that deter you, even if your first baguettes come out looking more like driftwood (as mine did). You can always cut up your experiments for bruschetta, so you will never be disappointed. All this to say, never give up! This also makes a fantastic pizza dough.

MAKES 4 TO 6 BAGUETTES

PREP TIME: 25 minutes (10 minutes to mix the dough, 5 minutes to knead the dough, and 10 minutes to divide and shape the dough)

INACTIVE TIME: 12 to 16 hours to pre-ferment the poolish, 1 hour to rest, 2 hours to rise, 45 minutes to proof the dough and preheat the oven

BAKE TIME: 20 to 25 minutes

TOOLS NEEDED: large container with lid, thermometer, kitchen scale, large bowl, kitchen towel or linen couche, 16-by-24-inch rimmed baking sheet, peel or wooden cutting board, roasting pan

FOR THE POOLISH
250 grams all-purpose flour
250 grams water
1 gram yeast

FOR THE DOUGH
3 grams instant yeast
680 grams water
1,000 grams all-purpose flour
20 grams salt

1. CREATE THE DOUGH: Follow the Master Recipe for Bread with Pre-ferment (page 112) through step 8, using the ingredient amounts listed.

2. RISE: Let the dough rise for 2 hours, making sure to fold it once at the 1-hour mark.

3. DIVIDE AND PRESHAPE: Divide the dough into 4 to 6 equal pieces, and let rest for 30 minutes.

4. SHAPE: Take 1 piece of dough and proceed with a letter fold, pressing the seal with the heel of the hand. This should leave you with a rectangular shape. Then take the top portion of dough that is far from you and fold it down to the center, pressing down with the heel of the hand, sealing the seam. Repeat, grabbing the far side of dough and pressing it, sealing it down to the center seam. Repeat one final time, tacking it down with the heel of the hand. You should have an elongated piece of dough. Lightly flour your hands and your work surface. Place a hand in the center of the dough and apply gentle pressure while rolling gently back and forth. Working with both hands, roll outward, tapering the ends of the baguette. Don't worry if this goes awkwardly at first; it takes lots of practice! Repeat with the other pieces of dough.

5. PROOF: Place the baguettes on a floured kitchen towel, creasing the fabric between each of the baguettes to separate them. Proof for 45 minutes, until puffy and airy and it feels like a marshmallow.

6. PREHEAT: While the dough is proofing, preheat the oven to 475°F. Place one oven rack in the highest position and the other in the middle position. Place an inverted baking sheet on the top rack, and place a roasting pan on the rack below. When pressed with a finger, it should leave an indent instead of springing back up.

7. BAKE: Transfer 3 or 4 baguettes to a heavily floured peel or wooden cutting board. Take your razor or lame and make a series of 3 slightly diagonal cuts down the center of each baguette, with each new slash starting just before the end of the previous one. Slide the baguettes onto the preheated baking sheet. Pour hot water into the roasting pan until it's about 1 inch deep. This will create steam. Bake for 10 minutes with steam, then carefully remove the roasting pan and bake another 10 to 15 minutes. The finished baguettes should be golden brown and will sound hollow when you thump them with your fingers. Repeat to bake the remaining baguettes.

8. COOL: Let cool on a wire rack for at least 30 minutes to let the interior crumb set and make it easier to slice.

Shaping, loading, and scoring poolish baguettes.

Boule with Biga

This recipe is another good starting point for incorporating a pre-ferment into your dough. The important thing to keep in mind is that the biga needs to be started at least 12 hours before you want to make bread. It doesn't require too much extra effort or time to do this; just a few minutes to mix it up, and then you can go on with your day. The flavor of bread made with a starter is well worth planning ahead.

MAKES 2 LOAVES

PREP TIME: 25 minutes (10 minutes to mix the dough, 5 minutes to knead the dough, and 10 minutes to divide and shape the dough)

INACTIVE TIME: 12 to 16 hours to pre-ferment the biga, 1 hour to rest, 3 hours to rise, 1 hour to 1 hour 30 minutes to proof the dough and preheat the oven

BAKE TIME: 40 to 45 minutes

TOOLS NEEDED: large container with lid, thermometer, kitchen scale, kitchen towel, large bowl, 2 round baskets, Dutch oven

FOR THE BIGA
200 grams all-purpose flour
150 grams water
¼ teaspoon instant yeast

FOR THE DOUGH
3 grams instant yeast
720 grams water
1,000 grams all-purpose flour
20 grams salt

CONTINUED →

1. CREATE THE DOUGH: Follow the Master Recipe for Bread with Pre-ferment (page 112) through step 8, using the ingredient amounts listed.

2. RISE: Let the dough rise for 3 hours, folding it once at the halfway point (about 1 hour 30 minutes in).

3. CHECK: After 3 hours, the dough should be larger and full of air. If you aren't sure, fill a cup with water, pinch off a little ball of your dough, and drop it into the glass. It should float to the top, indicating that your dough is aerated. Nice! If it doesn't seem particularly buoyant, it might be a cold day at your house. No worries. Let it rise a bit longer and check it again in 30 minutes or so.

4. DIVIDE AND PRESHAPE: Divide the dough in 2 equal pieces. Gently turn your dough onto a floured countertop. The bottom, which was in contact with the bowl, will be facing up to you. If it is sticking to the bowl, use your hand or a plastic scraper to release it. Shape the dough by giving it a gentle letter fold. Fold the far side (12 o'clock) down to the middle, sealing the dough against itself. Now fold the bottom up to meet the seam and seal it. Turn the dough so this seam is vertical, and do that letter fold again, sealing the dough to itself. You should have a nice little rounded square

shape. If the dough is nice and tight, you can stop there. If it seems very relaxed, you can give it another set of letter folds to create more tension, sealing the dough to itself.

5. BENCH REST: Rest the 2 pieces of dough on the work surface for 30 minutes. This will give them time to relax before shaping. Dust with flour and lightly cover with a kitchen towel.

6. SHAPE: Shape each piece into a boule. Flip the dough over and give it a letter fold, give it a quarter turn, and then give it another letter fold. Place the seam down and tighten up the loaf, pulling it against the work surface with your hands.

7. PROOF: Place your dough round into a basket lined with a floured kitchen towel, seam-side up. You are going to let this dough rise for 1 hour to 1 hour 30 minutes, until the dough feels airy, like a marshmallow. When pressed with a finger, it should leave an indent instead of springing back up. This is the final rise before it hops into the oven.

8. PREHEAT: While the dough is proofing, turn on your oven with an empty Dutch oven inside and let it preheat to 475°F. This may seem early to preheat the oven, but great bread needs a thoroughly hot oven for the best results.

9. CHECK: To test that the dough is well proofed, press a finger gently into the dough. If it seems springy and tight, it needs more time. If it feels airy and light, like a marshmallow, it's ready to bake. Needing more time for proofing is a common theme in baking bread. Don't let it worry you if your dough needs more time to rise! Feeling the dough and adapting to the timing needs every time you bake bread is the way to become a better baker, so let your senses guide you.

10. BAKE: Flour your work surface well and tip 1 loaf out of a basket onto it, seam-side down. Carefully pull your very hot Dutch oven out of the oven and place it on top of the stove with the lid next to it. Make 2 deep slashes in the top of the dough with a razor blade or lame, making a big X. This will allow your loaf to spring upward in all directions and rise while it bakes. Pick the dough up with your hands and gently drop it into the Dutch oven, and be careful to avoid burning your hands. Cover the Dutch oven with the lid, slide it into the oven, and bake for 25 minutes.

11. CHECK: At 25 minutes, take the cover off the Dutch oven. You should see a pale blond loaf that has risen to meet you. Continue baking with the cover removed for another 15 to 20 minutes. Your loaf will get some color and develop a nice crust. The finished loaf should be golden brown and will sound hollow when you thump it with your fingers. If the loaf seems to be browning too quickly, turn your oven down to 450°F. Repeat to bake the second loaf.

12. COOL: Let cool on a wire rack for at least 30 minutes to let the interior crumb set and make it easier to slice.

Ciabatta with Biga

Ciabatta gets its name from the Italian word for "slipper." It's a flattish bread with a large open crumb structure and crisp crust: truly magical for large, rustic sandwiches. The technique for this loaf is somewhat similar to the focaccia and ficelles from chapter 3. The wet dough should be handled gently to preserve the airy crumb. This dough will also make a lovely focaccia or fougasse if you like.

MAKES 4 CIABATTAS

PREP TIME: 20 minutes (5 minutes to mix the dough, 5 minutes to knead the bread, and 10 minutes to divide and shape the dough)

INACTIVE TIME: 12 to 16 hours to pre-ferment the biga, 30 minutes to rest, 2 hours to rise, 1 hour to proof the dough and preheat the oven

BAKE TIME: 40 to 45 minutes

TOOLS NEEDED: large container with lid, thermometer, kitchen scale, large bowl, kitchen towel, metal dough scraper, peel or wooden cutting board, baking sheet, roasting pan

FOR THE BIGA
200 grams all-purpose flour
160 grams water
¼ teaspoon instant yeast

FOR THE DOUGH
1,000 grams all-purpose flour
800 grams water
20 grams salt
4 grams instant yeast

CONTINUED →

1. CREATE THE DOUGH: Follow the Master Recipe for Bread with Pre-ferment (page 112) through step 7, using the ingredient amounts listed.

2. FOLD: Stretch and fold the dough, which will give it strength, so it can hold its shape in the oven later. Imagine that your dough has four "corners." Pull each corner up and stretch it over the top of the dough to meet the opposite side. Visualizing a clock on the top of your bowl of dough, pull the 12 o'clock corner up and down to 6. Pull the 3 o'clock over to 9, then the 6 o'clock up to 12, and the 9 o'clock over to 3. Work your way around the clock two or three times, until the dough becomes a tight ball and is no longer loose and stretchy.

3. RISE: Place a floured kitchen towel (or plastic wrap if that's what you have) over your bowl, and let rise for 1 hour. After 1 hour, give the dough a few folds, return it to the bowl, cover with the kitchen towel, and let it continue to rise for another hour.

4. DIVIDE AND PRESHAPE: Generously flour your work surface and carefully pull the dough out of the bowl. Gently pat the dough out with floured hands into a large rectangle. Use a dough scraper to cut 4 long rectangles about 10 by 4 inches each.

5. PROOF: Place the dough on a large, well-floured kitchen towel to rise for 1 hour.

6. PREHEAT: While the dough is proofing, preheat the oven to 475°F. Place one oven rack in the top position and the other in the middle of the oven. Place a baking sheet on the upper rack and a roasting pan on the middle rack.

7. BAKE: Gently place 1 piece of dough onto a floured peel or wooden cutting board and slide it onto the preheated baking sheet in the oven. Pour hot water into the roasting pan until it's about 1 inch deep. This will create steam. Bake with steam for 15 minutes. Carefully remove the roasting pan and bake for 5 more minutes. The finished ciabatta should be golden brown and will sound hollow when you thump it with your fingers. Repeat to bake the remaining dough.

8. COOL: Let cool on a wire rack for at least 30 minutes to let the interior crumb set and make it easier to slice. Brush off any excess flour.

Sourdough Starter

Creating your own sourdough starter is actually pretty straightforward despite the many myths and misconceptions that surround sourdough baking. There are a few considerations that need to be made, but a starter requires no more maintenance than a pet: It simply needs to be fed each day. Here are a few things that will ensure your success with sourdough:

FLOUR: Do not use bleached flour or low-quality flour. The flour is food for the wild yeast. Stone-milled whole-grain flour and unbleached flour provide the most nutrients for getting started.

WATER: Use filtered water when starting a new sourdough, since chlorinated water can deter the starter's development.

TEMPERATURE: Try not to subject your baby starter to extreme temperatures by keeping it too close to a stove (too hot) or near a drafty window (too cold). The perfect place to keep it is on a countertop where you will notice it and remember to feed it.

CONSISTENCY: Feeding the starter regularly is the most vital step to success. Try setting a recurring alarm on your phone as a reminder. I always feed mine before I go to bed, so it's just part of my evening routine.

ACTIVE TIME: A few minutes per day

INACTIVE TIME: 7 days

TOOLS NEEDED: kitchen scale, large plastic or glass container with lid

50 grams unbleached all-purpose flour
50 grams stone-milled
    whole-wheat flour
100 grams water

CONTINUED ➡

1. MIX: Combine the flour and water in a lidded container. Place the lid on top but leave it unsealed so that air can flow into the new starter. It should take 2 to 3 days to see signs of life from the starter.

2. FEED: When you see bubbles start to appear on the surface, it is time to begin feeding the starter. Remove half of the old starter and discard it. Then mix up more starter per the recipe. Repeat this feeding every day.

3. BAKE: By day 5, you should have a starter with lots of bubbles that should be rising vigorously. A strong, mature starter should have a sweet, almost fruity smell. When this happens, your starter is ready to make one of the bread recipes that follow. If it has a sour, alcohol aroma, throw it away and start over.

4. KEEP FEEDING: Each time you use your starter for baking, remember to keep a small portion, and continue to feed it according to the same ratios given previously. Starters can last for years if you feed them properly and consistently.

✦ Common Problems and FAQs ✦

Q: My starter made a few bubbles, but now it's not doing anything. Is it dead?

A: This is pretty typical. Just give it a little more time, and continue feeding it!

Q: My starter seems to rise extremely slowly. Why is it so sluggish?

A: It might be too cold. Aim to keep your starter between 75°F and 80°F to help improve its vitality and strength.

Q: My starter smells very sour or is starting to smell like alcohol. Why?

A: This is an indication that the starter needs to be fed more often. (It has eaten all its "food" and has started producing alcohol.) It can also be a sign that the starter is too warm. Try feeding it cooler water and finding a cooler area for it to live.

Beginner's Sourdough Loaf

This is an adaptation of the first sourdough formula I began working with. The most important lessons I learned about working with sourdough are ones you have already learned by working your way through this book. The last piece of the puzzle is the health of the starter, which is by far the most important key to producing consistently great sourdough bread. The only way to have a vigorous, healthy starter is with consistent feeding and care. The other important factor is the leaven being ready to use: full of bubbles and doubled in size. Putting it all together takes practice, just like anything else. This is a lower-hydration dough that is easy to handle and work with, with a good amount of pre-ferment to keep the timeline shorter.

MAKES 2 LOAVES

PREP TIME: 25 minutes (10 minutes to mix the dough, 5 minutes to knead the dough, and 10 minutes to divide and shape the dough)

INACTIVE TIME: 12 hours to prepare the starter, 1 hour to rest, 3 hours to rise, 1 to 2 hours to proof the dough and preheat the oven

BAKE TIME: 40 to 45 minutes

TOOLS NEEDED: large plastic or glass container with lid, thermometer, kitchen scale, large bowl, 2 round baskets, 2 kitchen towels, Dutch oven

FOR THE STARTER
50 grams mature Master Recipe for Sourdough Starter (page 131)
150 grams all-purpose flour
150 grams water

FOR THE DOUGH
1,000 grams all-purpose flour
680 grams water
20 grams salt

CONTINUED →

1. MIX THE STARTER: To prepare the starter, combine the mature starter, flour, and water in a large container with a lid at least 12 hours before you plan to start mixing your dough. The container should have adequate space for the starter to double in size. Cover loosely with the lid.

2. CHECK: After 12 hours, check to see if your starter is full of air and has doubled in size. If you aren't sure if it's ready, use the "float test." Drop a small piece of dough into a glass of water to see if it floats. If it doesn't float, the starter needs more time to develop.

3. PREPARE: Find the ambient temperature of your kitchen with a thermometer. A great way to do this is to take the temperature of your flour while it is sitting out at room temperature. Take a look at the chart on page 21 to see what temperature water you need for your dough. I find the easiest way to get my water to the correct temperature is to fill a pitcher or jar with hot water and one with cold water from the tap. I pour the cold water into the hot water until I've reached the ideal temperature. The desired dough temperature here is 76°F.

4. SCALE: Weigh all of the ingredients separately before you begin. This helps keep everything accurate. Use smaller bowls for ingredients in smaller amounts to get the most precise reading.

5. COMBINE: To make the dough, combine the prepared starter, water, flour, and salt. I like to use my hands, or use a plastic dough scraper to help mix. The ingredients should come together easily and produce a wet but firm dough.

6. REST: Let your dough relax for about 30 minutes so the flour can absorb the water a bit, which will make it easier to knead.

7. KNEAD: Flour your work space and scrape the dough out onto it. Push forward into your dough with the heels of your hands, and then fold the elongated dough back toward you. Give the dough a quarter turn, then push the dough away and fold it back again. Keep kneading until you can feel that the dough has tightened up and has gotten smoother, usually about 10 minutes.

8. RISE: Place a floured kitchen towel (or plastic wrap if that's what you have) over your bowl, and let the dough rise for 3 hours. Halfway through the rise (after 1 hour 30 minutes), give it a few letter folds.

9. CHECK: After 3 hours, the dough should be lively, aerated, and buoyant. If you aren't sure, fill a cup with water, pinch off a little ball of your dough, and drop it into the glass. It should float to the top, indicating that your dough is aerated. If it doesn't seem particularly buoyant, it might be a cold day at your house. No worries. Let it rise a bit longer and check it again in 30 minutes or so.

10. DIVIDE AND PRESHAPE: Divide the dough into 2 equal pieces. Gently turn your dough onto a floured countertop. The bottom, which was in contact with the bowl, will be facing up to you. If it is sticking to the bowl, use your hand or a plastic scraper to release it. Shape the dough by giving it a gentle letter fold: Fold the far side (12 o' clock) down to the middle, sealing the dough against itself. Now fold the bottom up to meet the seam and seal it. Turn the dough so this seam is vertical, and do that letter fold again, sealing the dough to itself. You should have a nice little rounded square shape. If the dough is nice and tight, you can stop there. If it seems very relaxed, you can give it another set of letter folds to create more tension, sealing the dough to itself.

11. BENCH REST: Rest the 2 pieces of dough on the work surface for 30 minutes. This will give them time to relax before shaping. Dust with flour and lightly cover with a kitchen towel.

12. SHAPE: Shape each piece into a boule. Flip the dough over and give it a letter fold, give it a quarter turn, and then give it another letter fold. Place the seam down and tighten up the loaf, pulling it against the work surface with your hands.

13. PROOF: Place each dough round into a proofing basket lined with a floured kitchen towel, seam-side up. You are going to let this dough rise for 1 to 2 hours. This is the final rise before it hops into the oven.

14. PREHEAT: While the dough is proofing, turn on your oven with an empty Dutch oven inside and let it preheat to 475°F. This may seem early to preheat the oven, but great bread needs a thoroughly hot oven for the best results.

15. CHECK: To test that the dough is well proofed, press a finger gently into the dough. If it seems springy and tight, it needs more time. If it feels airy and light, like a marshmallow, it's ready to bake. Don't let it worry you if your dough needs more time to rise. Feeling the dough and adapting to the timing needs every time you bake bread is the way to become a better baker, so let your senses guide you.

CONTINUED →

16. BAKE: Flour your work surface well and tip 1 loaf out of a basket onto it, seam-side down. Carefully pull your very hot Dutch oven out of the oven and place it on top of the stove with the lid next to it. Make 2 deep slashes in the top of the dough with a razor blade or lame, making a big X. This will allow your loaf to expand upward in all directions and rise while it bakes without tearing. Pick the dough up with your hands and gently drop it into the Dutch oven, seam-side down, and be careful to avoid burning your hands. Cover the Dutch oven with the lid, slide it into the oven, and bake for 25 minutes.

17. CHECK: At 25 minutes, take the cover off the Dutch oven. You should see a pale blond loaf that has risen to meet you. Continue baking with the cover removed for another 15 to 20 minutes. Your loaf will get some color and develop a nice crust. The finished loaf should be golden brown and will sound hollow when you thump it with your fingers. If the loaf seems to be browning too quickly, turn your oven down to 450°F. Repeat to bake the second loaf.

18. COOL: Let cool on a wire rack for at least 30 minutes to let the interior crumb set and make it easier to slice.

Common Problems and FAQs

Q: My loaf didn't have a good rise or took very long to rise.

A: If you have practiced through this whole book and had some success, you should have a firm grasp on the key components of making a loaf. At this point, it all comes down to fine-tuning the starter process and building your intuition with the starter. The key to keeping your starter lively, refreshed, and strong is to be consistent in both the feeding schedule and the temperatures you're using. These will be the keys to finding success with your sourdough loaves.

Q: Why is my loaf heavy and dense?

A: This also goes back to the health of the starter. Remember that in sourdough bread, the starter does all the heavy lifting. Keeping it happy is the best way to improve the final product. Keep an eye on your starter and try to use it when it is at its peak (full of bubbles, doubled in size). Using the starter when it has collapsed and started to sour won't produce the best results. It takes time to get the hang of it, so keep trying!

Q: How can I get a more pronounced grigne, or "ear," on my loaf?

A: Two things can help with this: shaping nice and tight, and getting a deep score at a low blade angle to the loaf. On a batard, try holding the blade at barely a 10-degree angle off the surface of the loaf and giving a strong, deep slash down the length of the loaf. This takes lots of practice, but after many loaves, you will nail it.

Intermediate Folded Sourdough

This is a wetter dough with a smaller quantity of starter and a longer fermentation. You might notice that this reminds you of the no-knead doughs or the ciabatta dough. This dough produces a more nuanced flavor and a moist, open crumb. It takes a little more work since it requires additional folds to develop, but the payoff is definitely worth it.

MAKES 2 LOAVES

PREP TIME: 25 minutes (10 minutes to mix the dough, 5 minutes to knead the dough, and 10 minutes to divide and shape the dough)

INACTIVE TIME: 12 hours to prepare the starter, 5 hours to rise, 30 minutes to rest, 1 to 2 hours to proof the dough and preheat the oven

BAKE TIME: 40 to 45 minutes

TOOLS NEEDED: large plastic or glass container with lid, thermometer, kitchen scale, large bowl, 2 round baskets, 2 kitchen towels, Dutch oven

FOR THE STARTER
50 grams mature Master Recipe for
   Sourdough Starter (page 131)
50 grams all-purpose flour
50 grams whole-wheat flour
100 grams water

FOR THE DOUGH
850 grams all-purpose flour
150 grams whole-wheat flour
720 grams water
20 grams salt

1. PREPARE THE STARTER: Combine the mature starter, all-purpose flour, whole-wheat flour, and water in a large container with a lid at least 12 to 16 hours before you plan to start mixing your dough. The container should have adequate space for the starter to double in size. Cover the bowl loosely with the lid.

2. CHECK: After 12 hours, check to see if your starter is full of air and has doubled in size. If you aren't sure if it's ready, use the "float test." Drop a small piece of the starter into a glass of water to see if it floats. If it doesn't float, it needs more time to develop.

3. PREPARE: Find the ambient temperature of your kitchen with a thermometer. A great way to do this is to take the temperature of your flour while it is sitting out at room temperature. Take a look at the chart on page 21 to see what temperature water you need for your dough. I find the easiest way to get my water to the correct temperature is to fill a pitcher or jar with hot water and one with cold water from the tap. I pour the cold water into the hot water until I've reached the ideal temperature. The desired dough temperature here is 75°F.

4. SCALE: Weigh all of the ingredients separately before you begin. This helps keep everything accurate. Use smaller bowls for ingredients in smaller amounts to get the most precise reading.

5. COMBINE: To make the dough, combine the prepared starter, water, flour, and salt. I like to use my hands, or use a plastic dough scraper to help mix. The ingredients should come together easily and produce a wet but firm dough.

6. FOLD: Stretch and fold the dough, which will give it strength, so it can hold its shape in the oven later. Imagine that your dough has four "corners." Pull each corner up and stretch it over the top of the dough to meet the opposite side. Visualizing a clock on the top of your bowl of dough, pull the 12 o'clock corner up and down to 6. Pull the 3 o'clock over to 9, then the 6 o'clock up to 12, and the 9 o'clock over to 3. Work your way around the clock two or three times, until the dough becomes a tight ball and is no longer loose and stretchy. Place in a large bowl.

7. RISE: Place a floured kitchen towel (or plastic wrap if that's what you have) over your bowl. Every 20 minutes for the first 2 hours 20 minutes of rising time, give the dough a fold before returning it to the bowl. This will help continue to develop the dough.

8. CHECK: After 5 hours, the dough should be aerated and buoyant. If you aren't sure, fill a cup with water, pinch off a little ball of your dough, and drop it into the glass. It should float to the top, indicating that your dough is aerated. If it doesn't seem particularly buoyant, it might be a cold day at your house. No worries. Let it rise a bit longer and check it again in 30 minutes or so.

9. DIVIDE AND PRESHAPE: Divide the dough into 2 equal pieces. Gently turn your dough onto a floured countertop. The bottom, which was in contact with the bowl, will be facing up to you. If it is sticking to the bowl, use your hand or a plastic scraper to release it. Shape the dough by giving it a gentle letter fold: Fold the far side (12 o'clock) down to the middle, sealing the dough against itself. Now fold the bottom up to meet the seam and seal it. Turn the dough so this seam is vertical, and do that letter fold again, sealing the dough to itself. You should have a nice little rounded square shape. If the dough is nice and tight, you can stop there. If it seems very relaxed, you can give it another set

CONTINUED →

of letter folds to create more tension, sealing the dough to itself.

10. REST: Rest the 2 pieces of dough on the work surface for 30 minutes. This will give them time to relax before shaping. Dust with flour and lightly cover with a kitchen towel.

11. SHAPE: Shape each piece into a boule. Flip the dough over and give it a letter fold, give it a quarter turn, and then give it another letter fold. Place the seam down and tighten up the loaf, pulling it against the work surface with your hands.

12. PROOF: Place each dough round into a proofing basket lined with a floured kitchen towel, seam-side up. You are going to let this dough proof for 1 to 2 hours. This is the final rise before it hops into the oven.

13. PREHEAT: While the dough is proofing, turn on your oven, place an empty Dutch oven inside, and let it preheat to 475°F. This may seem early to preheat the oven, but great bread needs a thoroughly hot oven for the best results.

14. CHECK: To test that the dough is well proofed, press a finger gently into the dough. If it seems springy and tight, it needs more time. If it feels airy and light, like a marshmallow, it's ready to bake. Don't let it worry you if your dough needs more time to rise. Feeling the dough and adapting to the timing needs every time you bake bread is the way to become a better baker, so let your senses guide you.

15. BAKE: Flour your work surface well and tip 1 loaf out of a basket onto it, seam-side down. Carefully pull your very hot Dutch oven out of the oven and place it on top of the stove with the lid next to it. Make 2 deep slashes in the top of the dough with a razor blade or lame, making a big X. This will allow your loaf to expand upward in all directions and rise while it bakes without tearing. Pick the dough up with your hands and gently drop it into the Dutch oven, seam-side down, and be careful to avoid burning your hands. Cover the Dutch oven with the lid, slide it into the oven, and bake for 25 minutes.

16. CHECK: At 25 minutes, take the cover off the Dutch oven. You should see a pale blond loaf that has risen to meet you. Continue baking with the cover removed for another 15 to 20 minutes. Your loaf will get some color and develop a nice crust. The finished loaf should be golden brown and will sound hollow when you thump it with your fingers. If the loaf seems to be browning too quickly, turn your oven down to 450°F. Repeat to bake the second loaf.

17. COOL: Let cool on a wire rack for at least 30 minutes to let the interior crumb set and make it easier to slice.

Alchemy Sourdough

This is an adaptation of the loaf that I make at my own bakery, Alchemy Bread. It requires two separate starter procedures before mixing up the dough. I mill my own wheat flour the day before mixing my doughs, which gives this loaf a beautiful flavor. This is a loaf that is slowly fermented with sourdough, is highly hydrated, incorporates a healthy amount of whole grain, and strikes a middle ground between being a nutritious, grainy, crusty loaf and something airy enough to be accessible to new customers. Definitely work through the easier sourdough variations and get a handle on them before working up to this one. It's almost a full-time job to make, but it sure does draw a crowd!

MAKES 2 LOAVES

PREP TIME: 25 minutes (5 minutes to mix the dough, 10 minutes to fold the dough, and 10 minutes to divide and shape the dough)

INACTIVE TIME: 12 hours to prepare the starter, 5 hours to rise, 30 minutes to rest, 1 to 2 hours to proof the dough and preheat the oven

BAKE TIME: 40 to 45 minutes

TOOLS NEEDED: 2 large plastic or glass containers with lids, thermometer, kitchen scale, large bowl, 2 round baskets, 2 kitchen towels, Dutch oven

FOR THE STARTER
50 grams mature Master Recipe
    for Sourdough Starter (page 131)
75 grams whole-wheat flour
25 grams rye flour
100 grams water

FOR THE SECOND BUILD
100 grams mature Master Recipe
    for Sourdough Starter (page 131)
75 grams whole-wheat flour
25 grams rye flour
100 grams water

FOR THE DOUGH
500 grams all-purpose flour
200 grams bread flour
300 grams whole-wheat flour
780 grams water
22 grams salt

CONTINUED →

1. PREPARE THE STARTER: The night before (at least 12 hours before you plan to mix your dough), feed the starter as usual to prepare for baking: Combine the mature starter, whole-wheat flour, rye flour, and water in a large container with a lid. Cover the container loosely with the lid.

2. PREPARE THE SECOND BUILD: In the morning, combine the mature starter, whole-wheat flour, rye flour, and water in a large container with a lid at least 4 hours before you plan to start mixing your dough. The container should have adequate space for the starter to double in size. Cover the container loosely with the lid.

3. CHECK: Look at the starter and check to see if it is full of air and has doubled in size. If you aren't sure if it's ready, use the "float test." Drop a little piece of starter into a glass of water to see if it floats. If it doesn't float, they need more time to develop.

4. PREPARE: Find the ambient temperature of your kitchen with a thermometer. A great way to do this is to take the temperature of your flour while it is sitting out at room temperature. Take a look at the chart on page 21 to see what temperature water you need for your dough. I find the easiest way to get my water to the correct temperature is to fill a pitcher or jar with hot water and one with cold water from the tap. I pour the cold water into the hot water until I've reached the ideal temperature. The desired dough temperature here is 75°F.

5. SCALE: Weigh all of the ingredients separately before you begin. This helps keep everything accurate. Use smaller bowls for ingredients in smaller amounts to get the most precise reading.

6. COMBINE: To make the dough, combine the starter, second build, all-purpose flour, bread flour, whole-wheat flour, water, and salt. I like to use my hands, or use a plastic dough scraper to help mix. The ingredients should come together easily and produce a wet but firm dough.

7. FOLD: Stretch and fold the dough, which will give it strength, so it can hold its shape in the oven later. Imagine that your dough has four "corners." Pull each corner up and stretch it over the top of the dough to meet the opposite side. Visualizing a clock on the top of your bowl of dough, pull the 12 o'clock corner up and down to 6. Pull the 3 o'clock over to 9, then the 6 o'clock up to 12, and the 9 o'clock over to 3. Work your way around the clock two or three times, until the dough becomes a tight ball and is no longer loose and stretchy. Place in a large bowl.

8. RISE: Place a floured kitchen towel (or plastic wrap if that's what you have) over your bowl, and let rise for 5 hours. Every 20 minutes for the first 2 hours of rising time, give the dough a fold and return to the bowl. This will help continue to develop the dough.

9. CHECK: After 5 hours, the dough should be aerated and buoyant. If you aren't sure, fill a cup with water, pinch off a little ball of your dough, and drop it into the glass. It should float to the top, indicating that your dough is aerated. If it doesn't seem particularly buoyant, it might be a cold day at your house. No worries. Let it rise a bit longer and check it again in about 1 hour.

10. DIVIDE AND PRESHAPE: Divide the dough into 2 equal pieces. Gently turn your dough onto a floured countertop. The bottom, which was in contact with the bowl, will be facing up to you. If it is sticking to the bowl, use your hand or a plastic scraper to release it. Shape the dough by giving it a gentle letter fold: Fold the far side (12 o'clock) down to the middle, sealing the dough against itself. Now fold the bottom up to meet the seam and seal it. Turn the dough so this seam is vertical, and do that letter fold again, sealing the dough to itself. You should have a nice little rounded square shape. If the dough is nice and tight, you can stop there. If it seems very relaxed, you can give it another set of letter folds to create more tension, sealing the dough to itself.

11. REST: Rest the 2 pieces of dough on the work surface for 30 minutes. This will give them time to relax before shaping. Dust with flour and lightly cover with a kitchen towel.

12. SHAPE: Shape each piece into a boule. Flip the dough over and give it a letter fold, give it a quarter turn, and then give it another letter fold. Place the seam down and tighten up the loaf, pulling it across the work surface with your hands in a circular motion.

13. PROOF: Place each dough round into a proofing basket lined with a floured kitchen towel, seam-side up. You are going to let this dough proof for 1 to 2 hours. This is the final rise before it hops into the oven.

14. PREHEAT: While the dough is proofing, turn on your oven, place an empty Dutch oven inside, and let it preheat to 475°F. This may seem early to preheat the oven, but great bread needs a thoroughly hot oven for the best results.

15. CHECK: To test that the dough is well proofed, press a finger gently into the dough. If it seems springy and tight, it needs more time. If it feels airy and light, like a marshmallow, it's ready to bake. Don't let it worry you if your dough needs more time to rise. Feeling the dough and adapting to the timing needs every time you bake bread is the way to become a better baker, so let your senses guide you.

CONTINUED ➔

16.BAKE: Flour your work surface well and tip 1 loaf out of a basket onto it, seam-side down. Carefully pull your very hot Dutch oven out of the oven and place it on top of the stove with the lid next to it. Make 2 deep slashes in the top of the dough with a razor blade or lame, making a big X. This will allow your loaf to expand upward in all directions and rise while it bakes without tearing. Pick the dough up with your hands and gently drop it into the Dutch oven, seam-side down, and be careful to avoid burning your hands. Cover the Dutch oven with the lid, slide it into the oven, and bake for 25 minutes.

17.CHECK: At 25 minutes, take the cover off the Dutch oven. You should see a pale blond loaf that has risen to meet you. Continue baking with the cover removed for another 15 to 20 minutes. Your loaf will get some color and develop a nice crust. The finished loaf should be golden brown and will sound hollow when you thump it with your fingers. If the loaf seems to be browning too quickly, turn your oven down to 450°F. Repeat to bake the second loaf.

18.COOL: Let cool on a wire rack for at least 30 minutes to let the interior crumb set and make it easier to slice.

BOOKS

For more minimalist no-knead-style breads:
My Bread by Jim Lahey

For in-depth no-knead-style breads and pizzas:
Flour Water Salt Yeast by Ken Forkish

For more varieties of all kinds of flavored loaves with history and anecdotes:
The Bread Bible by Rose Levy Beranbaum

For kneaded sourdough breads in lots of flavors:
Breads from the La Brea Bakery by Nancy Silverton

For advanced sourdough enthusiasts:
Tartine Bread by Chad Robertson

For inspiring creativity in sourdough:
Sourdough by Sarah Owens

ONLINE

For wonderful resources for bread bakers of all levels:
The Bread Bakers Guild of America, www.BBGA.org

For tools, supplies, and well-vetted recipes:
King Arthur Flour, www.KingArthurFlour.com

For methodical explorations of sourdough baking:
Maurizio Leo's blog, www.ThePerfectLoaf.com

For travel and inspiring bread musings:
Sarah Owens's BK17 Bakery, www.BK17Bakery.com

Measurement Conversions

Volume Equivalents (Liquid)

STANDARD	US STANDARD (OUNCES)	METRIC (APPROXIMATE)
2 tablespoons	1 fl. oz.	30 mL
¼ cup	2 fl. oz.	60 mL
½ cup	4 fl. oz.	120 mL
1 cup	8 fl. oz.	240 mL
1½ cups	12 fl. oz.	355 mL
2 cups or 1 pint	16 fl. oz.	475 mL
4 cups or 1 quart	32 fl. oz.	1 L
1 gallon	128 fl. oz.	4 L

Oven Temperatures

FAHRENHEIT (F)	CELSIUS (C) (APPROXIMATE)
250°	120°
300°	150°
325°	165°
350°	180°
375°	190°
400°	200°
425°	220°
450°	230°

Volume Equivalents (Dry)

STANDARD	METRIC (APPROXIMATE)
⅛ teaspoon	0.5 mL
¼ teaspoon	1 mL
½ teaspoon	2 mL
¾ teaspoon	4 mL
1 teaspoon	5 mL
1 tablespoon	15 mL
¼ cup	59 mL
⅓ cup	79 mL
½ cup	118 mL
⅔ cup	156 mL
¾ cup	177 mL
1 cup	235 mL
2 cups or 1 pint	475 mL
3 cups	700 mL
4 cups or 1 quart	1 L

Weight Equivalents

STANDARD	METRIC (APPROXIMATE)
½ ounce	15 g
1 ounce	30 g
2 ounces	60 g
4 ounces	115 g
8 ounces	225 g
12 ounces	340 g
16 ounces or 1 pound	455 g

Recipe Index

Index

P

Peels, 18
Pizzas
  Pizza with Tomato and
    Mozzarella, 46–50
Pizza stones, 18
Poolish, 4, 10
  Baguettes with Poolish,
    120–122
  Bread with Pre-ferment
    (Poolish or Biga), 112–119
Pre-ferments, 10. See also
    Sourdough starter
  Baguettes with Poolish,
    120–122
  Boule with Biga, 124–127
  Bread with Pre-ferment
    (Poolish or Biga), 112–119
  Ciabatta with Biga,
    129–130
  troubleshooting, 121
Proofing, 4, 7
Proofing baskets, 4, 16

R

Raisins
  Cinnamon Raisin Swirl
    Bread, 92–94
  Country Raisin and Walnut
    Loaf, 66–69
Razor blades, 18

Record-keeping, 18
Rising, 6, 7. See also Proofing
Rosemary
  Rosemary and Lemon Zest
    Fougasse, 51–52

S

Salt, 2
Scaling, 4, 5
Scoring, 19
Shaping, 7, 57
Sourdough starter, 10
  Alchemy Sourdough,
    144–148
  Beginner's Sourdough
    Loaf, 135–138
  Intermediate Six-Fold
    Sourdough, 140–142
  master recipe, 131–132
  troubleshooting, 134, 139
Spring, 4, 7
Starters. See Sourdough
    starter
Straight dough, 10

T

Temperature
  air, 20, 21
  baking, 8
  calculations, 21
  water, 20, 21

Thermometers, 18
Time, 20
Tomatoes
  Pizza with Tomato and
    Mozzarella, 46–50
Troubleshooting
  enriched breads, 88
  kneaded breads, 62
  no-knead breads, 33
  pre-ferments, 121
  sourdough starter and
    breads, 134, 139

W

Water, 2, 20, 21
Weighing ingredients, 5, 16,
    20
Whole grain breads
  Brown Sugar Spice
    Oatmeal Bread, 76–79
  Country Parmesan and
    Black Pepper Loaf, 70–73
  Country Raisin and Walnut
    Loaf, 66–69
  Country Wheat Loaf
    Variation, 65
  Kindergarten Honey
    Wheat Bread, 74–75
Whole-grain flour, 3

Y

Yeast, 3

Acknowledgments

I'd like to thank my husband, Aaron, who lets me invite the whole town to our house every week and puts up with an insane quantity of dirty dishes, and me running a 500°F oven all hours of the night, without (much) complaint and has supported me through all of the ups and downs.

My kids, who have been unceasingly proud of me despite my many flaws and shortcomings, and constantly encourage me. My parents, who taught me to read and always took me to the library and encouraged me to write, which is how I eventually taught myself to bake. My friend Candace, who is simply the best in every way. My friend Michelle, who is such a great business mentor and encourages me to follow my passion. My friend Gillian, who has encouraged me and lent her grammatical expertise and thoughtful suggestions, and helped test many of the recipes. My friend Ellen, who sent me a postcard every week while I was writing this book to encourage me. My friend Emily, who brought me numerous coffees exactly the way I like them in moments of crisis. My friend Janelle, who took my kids on all kinds of adventures while I was busy working. My friend Amy, who is always first in line on Saturdays to get a baguette. My friend Ruhi, who was the very first person to buy a loaf of my bread. All my regular customers, who give me a reason to stay up all night baking; all my friends who have been there for me in big and small ways over the years, through good times and tough times; and all my fellow bakers on Instagram who leave thoughtful comments, share new recipes, and chat with our whole community of bakers about the ups and downs of baking life.

About the Author

BONNIE OHARA is a self-taught sourdough bread baker who has been perfecting her craft since 2010. With a background in literature and art, she comes to baking with a visual style and runs her company with a heart for storytelling. When she's not baking sourdoughs for Alchemy Bread in her 1920s bungalow, you can find her bicycling the trails with her three children, picking up veggies and fruit at the farmers' market, or checking out cookbooks and picture books at the library.